THE WIDOW'S MIGHT

THE WIDOW'S MIGHT

IS FOUND AT THE THRONE OF GRACE

EMBRACING THE BRIDEGROOM

by Marjorie Graham Osborne

XULON PRESS

Xulon Press
2301 Lucien Way #415
Maitland, FL 32751
407.339.4217
www.xulonpress.com

Unless otherwise indicated, Scripture quotations taken from the New American Standard Bible (NASB). Copyright © 1960, 1962, 1963, 1968, 1971, 1972, 1973, 1975, 1977, 1995 by The Lockman Foundation. Used by permission. All rights reserved.

Scripture quotations taken from the Amplified Bible Classic Edition (AMPC). Copyright © 1965, 1987 by The Lockman Foundation. Used by permission. All rights reserved.

Scripture quotations taken from the King James Version (KJV) – public domain.

Scripture quotations taken from the New King James Version (NKJV). Copyright © 1982 by Thomas Nelson, Inc. Used by permission. All rights reserved.

Printed in the United States of America.
Edited by Xulon Press.

Greek definitions are derived from Strong's Greek Concordance.

Hebrew definitions are derived from Strong's Hebrew Concordance

The cover is displayed against a backdrop of the eagle nebulae in honor of the 101st airborne and was designed by James Nesbit https://jnesbit.com/

ISBN-13: 9781545629390

WHAT LEADERS
ARE SAYING

I met the Osbornes in 1995 when they attended a Mahesh Chavda conference we hold each December in Austin Texas. We have been blessed by the great friendship that developed over the years with Margie and Nicky. I was honored to walk alongside them as friend and pastor spending many hours with them on the phone and in person. When Nicky received the report of his illness I watched how they fought the good fight of faith all the way to his homecoming. Being friends with them let me have a front row seat to this great struggle. When Nicky made his transition to Heaven, I cried and rejoiced at the same time. Officiating the homecoming service was one of the special times in my ministry life, rejoicing in a life well lived and the great testimony of Nicky's life on earth.

Margie's book, *The Widow's Might* is filled with direction and comfort for any one facing the great trial of loss. I will personally use what she has written to help those I pastor when they face similar challenge. I believe her heart felt testimony and counsel belongs in every pastor's library as a guide to minister to those in mourning. Let Margie guide you through the most difficult time any spouse faces in this life.

Bill Hart
Senior Pastor, Founder
Austin Cathedral
Austin , Texas

If God is doing something, Margie wants in. I first met her in 1990 and prayed for God to bring her a husband who was a man of God. When Nicky and she married they became an anointed ministry team, willing to go anywhere God called them to preach the gospel.

Because of her hunger for more of God, Margie has been on the cutting edge of the latest moves of God in our generation. Wherever Jesus is manifesting His presence through His Holy Spirit, Margie wants to be there. Usually she is. She is an incredible woman of faith and integrity. My wife, Sherry, and I count it a great honor to be her friend.

When Margie speaks, I listen. I encourage everyone to read what God has revealed to her in *The Widow's Might*. The strength she found at the throne of grace when Nicky left for Heaven is testimony to the power of God to heal and restore. Her story will draw everyone who reads it into a deeper relationship with Jesus Christ.

Max Greiner: Artist, Founder
Sculpture Prayer Garden Kerrville, Texas
www.thecomingkingfoundation.org/home.htm

WHAT WIDOWS ARE SAYING

I thought I was going crazy after John died until I talked with Margie. She shared some chapters from her book, and what she had written came alive. I had just experienced what had happened to her in the grocery store. Then I read what she had written about Heaven. My last words to John had been that this was going to be the first time in fifty years we wouldn't share everything. He was going to see Heaven, without me. It seemed like Margie's description of Heaven and what John was seeing were written by God especially for me. What a gift of comfort!

Peggy

Margie puts into words what most people don't know how to say. Her prayers were a great help to me because when I pray I have not known how to express what I am feeling. I could identify with everything she went through, and what she wrote about the foxes is helping me each day.

Marie

I couldn't put this book down. I could not wait to read the next step the Lord told Margie to take as He led her out of sorrow into new life. When you read *The Widow's Might* your mourning is changed to dancing as you are brought closer to Jesus and all His glory.

Betty

DEDICATION

It is with joy I dedicate this book to my Bridegroom Jesus Christ the Son of God.

He has turned for me my mourning into dancing. He has put off my sackcloth and clothed me with gladness, to the end that my glory may sing praise to Him and not be silent. While I dance before Him here on earth, Nicky dances before Him in Heaven. O Lord my God, I will give thanks to You forever! (from Psalm 30:11)

ACKNOWLEDGEMENTS

It seems that most often our Father's love and help comes to us through the wonderful people He sends into our lives. In gratitude to Him, I want to acknowledge and thank my daughter, Elizabeth, for her encouragement and hours of editing while caring for her three boys under the age of four. She is a super daughter and super mom. My thanks to her husband, Jamie, who was always there for me when it came to hugs and technical issues. His parents Jim and Cindi took me under their wing and into their home where I spent many hours writing. Thank you. My son, Adam, never failed to encourage me. His generosity and patience was a lifeline through many difficult days. Adam and my daughter, Rebekah, enthusiastically guiding me through cyberspace was invaluable; a mother could not have a better son and daughters. My thanks to Fritz Wolmarans who came to my rescue many times and honored me as though I was his own grandmother. My thanks to Charlene Miller, Pat Jordan, Ellen Booth, Betty Buffington and others who proof read manuscripts and cheered me on. Had it not been for the gracious encouragement of Anna Rountree who opened her door to me as a stranger, this book may not have come to completion. Her words were a beacon of light when all seemed lost.

Most of all I am grateful to our Father for the gift of my husband, Nicky Osborne, whose unconditional love for me and my children healed our broken hearts for seventeen wonderful years. His love created the foundation for us to go forward without him. Thank you, Nicky.

As he stepped through the veil I am sure he was greeted with the words, "Well done, My good and faithful servant."

TABLE OF CONTENTS

FOREWORD

*T*he great tragedy is that sooner or later we all face the heart-breaking loss of loved ones who have been the center of our world. The death of our parents or siblings, the unexpected and tragic loss of a child or the loss of our spouse--any of these losses present great challenges to living a life of faith without becoming bitter.

Widows often face the hardest road when they lose their husband and love of their life. *The Widow's Might* is filled with the real-life challenges many women face when they lose their mate. Their grief is often accompanied by financial crisis, and the sudden responsibility for things, making a living, and managing money. They must navigate these new arenas without their soulmate, their friend, and closest confidante to provide the stability of companionship and love as they live life from day to day.

I have known Margie for several decades and have watched how she has sought the Lord as a true worshiper, a faithful wife, and loving mother. When God sent Nicky Osborne into her life it was obvious he was a special man of God. It was wonderful to see them enter years of happiness as a ministry team preaching the gospel. Margie fought the good fight of faith after getting the news that her husband had cancer. She believed to the very end for his healing. It was hard for all of us who stood with her in prayer to see Nicky finish his course and go on to heaven.

In courageously writing *The Widow's Might* Margie takes us on a journey into the sudden and unknown world of not having her husband. She doesn't sugar coat the journey, but takes the challenge head on with all the hardship and heartache that accompany it.

I'm reminded of Jesus who came to identify with us in all our weakness and became like us in all things. He in turn wants us to identify with others. As you read *The Widow's Might* you may recognize your journey or identify the journey of someone who may need your help. Margie lays out the pain but doesn't leave us there. On every page, she weaves God's word into a beautiful portrait of how every widow can find a window of hope and love that leads her to freedom from the devastation of loss. As you read, let your heart take you from the depths and hard truth of loss to the mountain of victory through Jesus Christ. Hopefully by the time you have taken this journey with Margie you will appreciate and love her like Bonnie and I do.

Dr. Mahesh Chavda
Senior Pastor
All Nations Church
Charlotte, NC

INTRODUCTION

Our farm was my husband's dream come true while we planned for retirement. Glistening with dew, a new carpet of grass was springing up in the fields, and sprays of dogwood decorated the woods as towering trees put forth their leaves. Spring was in full celebration in Kentucky! Birds rejoiced in song and the crystal-clear pond rippled with activity. The clean country air was invigorating as I saddled my horse. Banner was eager for an early morning ride. A gift from my husband, he was a profound statement of beauty. A tall black and white Saddlebred, with a playful personality that betrayed his good looks.

Riding this elegant horse against the backdrop of God's glorious creation was exhilarating. It was my favorite time to sing praises to Jesus with Banner's gait setting the rhythm for my song. We clipped down the road past the neighboring farms in a fast, high-stepping trot. With his mane flying and his tail held high, joy filled the air.

Then suddenly, without warning, Banner stumbled and fell, and I was sent sailing over his head! It was the kind of fall that can cripple a horse and leave the rider paralyzed, if not dead. Instead, God's angels caught me as I flew forward. They tucked my chin down and spun me into a perfect somersault, landing me gently on the ground. I lay on my back looking up at the sky and Banner's nose while he stood looking down at me. He was unscathed as well! Undaunted, I rode back to the farm reveling in the living reality of God's Word. The only possible explanation for my not being injured was Psalm 37:23, 24.

"The steps of a man are established by the Lord, and He delights in his way. When he falls, he will not be hurled headlong because the Lord is the One who holds his hand."

Nicky was away from home on a job in Texas. He called in the evening and said he was alerted to pray for me that morning. He was concerned about my being alone at the farm, and I was happy to tell him about my miraculous rescue. There was nothing to fear with God's angels watching over me.[1]

Two years later my life took another unexpected fall designed to crush my spirit and shake my faith to the core. Again, God caught me, but this time getting up was much harder than getting back on a horse. Nicky was diagnosed with stage four cancer, and within a few months the love of my life was gone. My heart was broken, and our shared hopes and dreams were shattered. The wind was knocked out of me this time. I didn't doubt the goodness of God. I doubted myself and who I would prove to be. But once more, though I was fallen, I was not hurled headlong. Jesus took me by the hand, and He told me to keep a journal while He gently landed me back on my feet. He made it clear this book would be gleaned from its pages as an offering poured out for others.

It has not been easy to bare my heart before the world and admit the depths of my struggle, but as I attended a writer's conference, the Lord's commission became clear. They said what I already knew to be true. Our testimonies are designed for the comfort of others. Some will identify with my story as if it was written especially for them. My prayer is that *The Widow's Might* will be placed in their hands by God's providence. May they receive it as a gift from Jesus, written by the Holy Spirit with them in mind.

---

[1] Ps. 91:11,12

PART ONE

ENTERING THE WORLD OF WIDOWHOOD

"The righteous cry, and the Lord hears
and delivers them out of all their troubles.
The Lord is near to the brokenhearted
and saves those who are crushed in spirit"
(Psalm 34:17-19).

CHAPTER 1

THE WIDOW'S CRY

"I go about mourning without comfort; I stand up in the assembly and cry out for help" (Job 30:28).

I was at a televised Christian conference being held at the Fort Worth Convention Center in Texas. Thousands were assembled to hear a renowned minister speak. Suddenly, in the middle of his message, a woman started screaming hysterically in the balcony. Her shrill cries turned every eye toward her, and the ushers rushed to see what was wrong.

She was a widow crying out for help in heart-wrenching despair. Her husband had died eighteen months earlier, and she was destitute. She had nothing left but sorrow and grief after hospital bills had devoured their savings. Under the crushing weight of grief, anguish and poverty, she had collapsed. Hearing her story, I fully identified with her breaking point. I remembered what it felt like to be on the brink of crying out for help in the assembly like it says in Job 30:28.

Two years before, I cried uncontrollably face down on my office floor, overwhelmed by the problems I faced as a widow. It had been eighteen months since Nicky left for

Heaven, and I had spent that time traveling or staying with friends. It was easier to deal with grief away from the memories of our home. When I returned to our farm to prepare it for sale, however, I was hit with fresh waves of grief all over again. Sorting through Nicky's things and going through our closet was heartbreaking. Moreover, something had gone terribly wrong in my absence; the house smelled so horrible I could barely spend a night there. The rank odor was coming from under the house, but none of the contractors I called had identified the problem.

Finally I mustered the courage to crawl under the house to see what the problem was. As I crept along, on my belly in some places, muttering thoughts ran through my mind, "A woman shouldn't have to do this. Certainly, *at my age*, no woman would even *consider* doing this." Then it ran in another direction: "I can do this. I'll figure this out myself." So, fighting grief and waving aside spider webs, I bravely pushed forward in the dirt crawl space. What I found was devastating. The earth was washed away under the foundation, and water was standing in stagnant pools in the dugout tornado shelter.

All courage fled from me! After coming out from under the house, I lay on my office floor crying uncontrollably, my body racked with sobs. Feeling lost without Nicky to solve the problem and drowning in waves of grief, I was collapsing. "Lord, I need my husband!" I bellowed from the anguish in my soul. God's still small voice said, "Trust Me," but I listened to the storm of despair instead.

I was watching my finances vanish overnight. Everything depended on selling the farm, and now it was impossible to put it on the market. Fear crowded against me. I was under a hammering bombardment. "Abba, Father," I cried out, "I need help!"

The phone rang. It was a friend from Ohio saying, "Margie, I have been praying for you, and the Lord caused me to feel

4

what you are feeling. You should not be alone right now." She was coming to stay with me for a while. Finally someone knew what I was going through! She was experiencing it. God was letting her feel it. For some reason, with that knowledge, relief washed over me.

That's what Jesus did. He came down here and felt all our pain, suffering and anguish. He took on the despair of the world, and He cried out from the cross what had been seeping from my heart: "My God, my God, why hast thou forsaken me?" (Mark 15:34b, KJV) He knew the barrenness of the emotional wilderness I was in. He knew my exhaustion. I had been afraid He wasn't coming through for me, even though He always had before, and He understood it all. I was disappointed in myself for not trusting Him, but He didn't care about my failure. He was sending me help.

I got through the foundation repairs, but what I thought would take a month to get the farm ready for sale turned into a year. As more problems arose, it became a year of learning to trust God through things that seemed impossible. Later I asked the Lord, "Why did You allow such a long season of trouble? I have been through so much!"

He replied,

> "How will you comfort My widows whose tears are never imagined by those who love them, unless you experience it? Unless you walk in hard places, how can you encourage those who are overwhelmed? My widows need to know the road they are on is well traveled, and they can trust Me to come through for them. Moreover, I want My people awakened to the high calling of helping widows. How will they know their needs unless you write the words My widows will never voice to others?"

Nicky and I cared for widows throughout our ministry, but when I joined their ranks I was stunned to realize how little we knew about them. I discovered their world to be a place of surreal grief and problems beyond description, and I regretted we had not done more for them. Thus, I write this book with a passion to comfort them more effectively and to assure them of God's love. Each widow's situation is different, but many are weeping behind closed doors in need of help and moral support. Their tears rend the heart of God.

James 1:27 says, "This is pure and undefiled religion in the sight of our God and Father, to visit orphans and widows in their distress." The word translated "visit" means more than one would suppose. It means *to select, go see, relieve and look out for.* God is looking for those who are willing to protect and befriend His widows. He is looking for those willing to be used by Him as He tenderly cares for these precious ones who are so close to His heart. Therefore, with our Father's compassion for widows in mind, come with me while I share my story. I believe what God taught me as He carried me through the most difficult season of my life will help and encourage others.

I will begin with the day my husband went to Heaven in the next chapter, followed by a profound encounter with God's love that took place a few days later. Through these two dramatic events God showed me *His perspective,* and He made it clear I must adopt *His point of view.* Seeing things the way He sees them was a critical step to recovering from my loss and overcoming what lay ahead of me.

Therefore, to help us "look up" and set our minds on God's perspective, I have written what took place on earth the day Nicky stepped into eternity mixed with possible scenes from Heaven. What happened in the physical world is viewed alongside the invisible, as spun from my imagination. After all, we know with certainty, what took place was being watched from above and recorded in Heaven. According to the Scriptures, all the days of our lives are being chronicled in God's book of remembrance by angelic scribes.[2] How closely will my story align with what the angels have written? When we go to Heaven we can read the books, and we will see!

---

[2] Mal. 3:16, Ps. 139:16, Ps. 103:20, 21

CHAPTER 2

NICKY'S GREATEST DAY

**"Precious (important and no light matter) in
the sight of the Lord is the death of His saints
(His loving ones)" (Psalm 116:15, AMPC).**

November 9, 2012, was the most amazing and highly
honored day of Nicky Osborne's life. Saturated with
the glory of God, the day was planned and foreknown by our
Creator from the foundation of the world.[3] Everyone coming
into the hospital room could feel the tangible presence of
the Holy Spirit as worship and music ascended before the
throne of God. Anticipation filled the air. I refused to listen
to anything but the heartbeat of God, and His heartbeat was,
"Celebrate! Celebrate! Celebrate!" Praising God in celebration
of His great love had become the fabric of our lives. Nicky
and I knew the powerful reality of God inhabiting the praises
of His people.[4] I worshipped and sang relentlessly, inviting
His presence.

---

[3] Ps. 139
[4] Ps. 22:3

The night before, Nicky's friend Mark had come to read the Scriptures to him. Even though he was in a coma, we knew Nicky could hear him while he read for hours, filling the room with the Word of God. After midnight, Mark was impressed by the Holy Spirit to read Ezekiel 39:8. It said, "Behold, it is come, and it is done, saith the Lord God; this is the day whereof I have spoken" (KJV). There was a God-given assurance that, in fact, this was the day our prayers would be answered as indicated by Ezekiel 39.

From early morning to evening, I held on to hope and sang and worshipped with resolute celebration before Jesus. Hundreds of people on prayer chains were praying with me for my husband to be healed. Was it going to happen? Nick and I weren't strangers to last-minute miracles.

He had gone to the edge of death several times before. Once, before we met, he tried to end his life as a hopeless drug addict with a massive cocaine overdose. His heart pounded wildly as he lay dying, but an angel in brilliant light came in the room. He reached into Nicky's chest, saying, "I'm not going to let you die, Nicky! I am holding your heart, and you are going to live." Later, as he answered the call on his life to preach the gospel and was delivered from addiction, Nicky and I met and were married. Together we lived a supernatural life serving Jesus; to us, miracles were normal. But this time I knew God was giving Nicky a choice. He could go to Heaven if he wanted to.

For a week he had been closed in with God, unresponsive to the physical world; but in his spirit he was alert and attentive to His Father's voice. I knew he had gone somewhere with Him in the supernatural realm more than once.[5] At one point, I was amazed to see his feet moving as if he were walking somewhere. What was being revealed to him as he

---

[5]   2 Cor. 12:2, 2 Kings 5:26, Ezek. 40:2

hovered on the edge of eternity? Was he deciding to stay here a while longer, or did he long for Heaven?

The room was crowded with the invisible. Angels were in attendance, resplendent in their glistening robes, and thousands joyfully peered through the heavenly portal opened to the hospital room. This was "the cloud of witnesses" who watch us from Heaven's dimension as we run our race.[6] Among them were Nicky's parents, childhood friends, his daughter, granddaughter, great granddaughter, and his son, Dean. My parents made their way to the front row.

Crowding the portal were hundreds of men whose lives had been extended through Nicky's rescue missions with the 101st Airborne in Vietnam. Two Bronze Stars told the story of Nicky's valor during the war. Five-star general Omar Bradley and four-star general Ralph Haines joined those looking in. General Haines had entertained Nicky in his home where they had shared their mutual passion for Jesus. General Bradley remembered Nicky as a member of his personal flight crew in the later years of his life. They'd had many conversations as a father to a son.

The crowd swelled in number as word spread in Heaven. "This is the day!" A group of excited ladies made their way through the joyous throng to take their place at the portal balcony. They were the widows Nicky had cared for at the little country church we pastored. We left there to minister in the Texas prisons, and some of the prisoners were at the portal too. Through Nicky, they had made it out of darkness into the kingdom of God. They couldn't wait to greet him.

Back in the hospital room, the atmosphere was thick with the glory of God. Anticipation mounted as the day advanced toward evening.

"Now!"

---

[6] Heb.12:1 Note: I capitalize 3rd Heaven as a proper noun.

The signal was given! In an instant Nicky was freed from his body and viewing the hospital room from above the bed. I looked up wondering if he was watching me. Under the full gaze of his Father, he was in light as never before. He was enveloped in total love and freedom far beyond the reach of any contamination of the fallen world, and he was alive. He was wonderfully alive!

The music playing on the CD player in the room came to life and dance all around him. Loosed from the dimension of time, the music turned into dazzling colors moving in rhythmic waves of light.[7] In awe he wondered, "Is this what God sees when we sing to Him?" Added to it were heavenly voices and notes and instruments, of which the earthly music was only a shadow.

Then suddenly, Nicky's escort arrived. Attending escort angels and warring angels in magnificent array ushered Nicky onto the transport craft.[8] It beat anything he had imagined when he had wondered about his departure. It appeared to be solid yet was made of light and fire.[9] All was fiery light!

In a flashing surge of power, Nicky was streaking through the first heaven and penetrating the second heaven at a speed far beyond the speed of light. The escort angels garrisoned around the craft, forming a shield. Others transformed into fierce war machines and weaponry as they cut a swath through the second heaven where the thrones of renegade princes and wicked spirits in high places reeled and careened at their passage. The evil horde scrambled to mount a counter offensive, but they were no match for God's elite warring host. The vast spiritual war between the kingdom of God and satan and his fallen angels recorded in the Bible, sprang to life before him. "We wrestle not against flesh and blood, but against principalities, against powers, against the rulers of the darkness of

---

[7] Inspired by stories of people who have reported seeing Heaven.
[8] Inspired by Ezek.1.
[9] Inspired by 2 Kings 2:11.

this world, against spiritual wickedness in high places." (Eph. 6:12, KJV).

He sped past the planets and stars in breathless wonder marveling at the electric color display of nebulae as he traversed one galaxy after another. Mounting higher and higher, the craft streaked toward the grand reception awaiting him at Heaven's gate. God's goodness was amazing. In the past months, Nicky had watched documentaries viewing the universe through the Hubble telescope. He was awestruck by the vastness of space and the power of our Father and Creator who, by the faintest whisper of His voice, had spoken trillions of planets and stars into existence.[10] Now he was seeing it firsthand! Moreover, he was on his way to meet this God of love face-to-face. It was more than he could fathom!

He looked to his left in astonishment. Piloting the craft was his friend, Sam, who had been killed in Vietnam. Nicky had flown with him as his gunner pilot on their numerous rescue missions with the Screaming Eagles of the 101st Airborne. "Welcome aboard, Osborne. This sure beats a Huey helicopter, doesn't it? O death, where is your sting, eh?"[11] They burst into joyous laughter, and Sam accelerated for a detour through the Eagle Nebula in honor of their days with the Screaming Eagles. What a ride! The Father was laughing from His throne, and a throng gathered at the gate as the witnesses rushed from the viewing portal to the reception area where Nicky was about to arrive.

Meanwhile, I lingered in the hospital room. I could feel the glory of God and the presence of the angels who had been called in for this grand occasion: Nicky's Greatest Day. I was worshipping Jesus the first time Nicky saw me at a little country church in Texas, and now I was worshipping as he left for Heaven. Grace and peace rested on me.

---

[10] Job 26:14, AMPC
[11] See 1Cor. 15:55

In perfect timing, a friend "just happened" to stop by the hospital. He helped me gather my belongings, but when we got to the parking garage the battery in my car was dead. He charged the battery for me, loaded the car and checked me into a hotel down the street. I thought to myself, "What a mess I would be in without this help. Thank You, Father. I don't know how I would have handled this alone in the middle of the night."

He whispered to me,

> "Remember—and don't forget—I will always
> send you all the help you need."

Peace surrounded me as I established Heaven's boundary in the hotel room by playing my worship music. It seemed to me that Nicky was still nearby. I lay down and slept as I breathed my most familiar prayer: "Father, give me grace. Give me strength. This is going to take a lot of grace, Father. Help me."

With the arrival of a new day, as dawn was breaking over the landscapes of Kentucky, I knew it wasn't time to be engulfed in plans for a memorial service. My whole world had changed. I needed to get my bearings and hear clearly from the Lord before I did anything. I couldn't imagine life without Nicky, and the last three weeks at the hospital had been exhausting. I needed to rest and retreat in prayer to gain strength.

I asked family members to spend the week reflecting on the life of this remarkable man whose life we had shared. Jesus had touched all of us with His love through Nicky Osborne.

CHAPTER 3

THE FIERY LOVE OF GOD

"How precious is Your steadfast love, O God! The children of men take refuge and put their trust under the shadow of Your wings" (Psalm 36:7, AMPC).

$\mathcal{A}$s I worshipped at the hotel the Holy Spirit embraced me in the warmth of His love, and I felt the presence of angels guarding me.[12] I didn't want to leave this secret place close to the heart of God prematurely.[13] Going home without Nicky was going to be very hard, and the fact that he was gone was beginning to sink in. From the deepest part of my being I prayed, "Father, this is going to take a lot of grace. Help me!"

As I continued worshipping for several days, the presence of God intensified in the room until the atmosphere became so charged with His glory I could barely speak. The room became hazy, and I realized I was in the cloud of His manifest presence.[14] Something dramatic was about to happen. I

---

[12] Heb. 1:13, 14
[13] Ps. 91:1
[14] 1 Kings 8:10

crossed the room and sat down on the couch in wide-eyed wonder; I knew I was on the edge of something extraordinary. The atmosphere was electric! "Lord, what is happening?" I waited for an explanation; but there was only peace and silence, and I fell into a deep sleep.

Suddenly, at three o'clock in the morning, I was jolted wide awake by a wonderful fiery hot supernatural love, blazing upon my heart. It burned and flared against my chest for just a moment with an intensity I thought would kill me. I almost couldn't bear it! But it was amazing and wonderful at the same time. It was the pure and holy love that pours like a river of fire from the heart of God, enveloping all His sons and daughters in Heaven. It was incredible! Impossible to describe! Only those in Heaven with spiritual bodies can endure its full force without perishing.

The encounter was a profound experience and an amazing gift from God. The message it left emblazoned upon my heart was:

> "Taste where Nicky is, Margie. Taste the atmo-
> sphere of My love in Heaven that now burns in
> his heart for you, and don't forget it. This love
> is far greater than the love you shared on earth,
> and it shines on you from above every day."

God was answering my prayers for grace to go home to the farm. It was going to be difficult, but the compass given to me in that fiery experience of God's love was clearly defined. I was to keep my mind riveted on the reality of eternity and the overpowering love that emanates from the heart of God. It was to be a treasure in my heart, directing my steps in the future. A warning to keep my eyes and heart fixed on things above, awaiting my Greatest Day when it would be my turn to step into Heaven and be held in the arms of my Creator. Nicky and all our loved ones who have gone before us bask in this fiery love. They can bear its full flame and power because they are no longer confined to earthbound bodies. This love burns bright in their hearts for us while they watch us finish our race, awaiting the day we will join them, never to be separated again.

I packed my bags and headed home. It was time to plan for Nicky's memorial service. Peace rested on me as I drove to our farm. But when I pulled into the driveway, the playing field changed. I was struck with the cold reality of Nicky's absence, and mourning and grief set in with a cloud burst of tears.

Now I would begin my journey into a deeper relationship with Jesus than I had known before, and He would show me the way out of sorrow and mourning. I would learn to keep my "mind set on things above" and stay focused on God's amazing love for me as I went forward. God would direct me each step of the way.

CHAPTER 4

THE THRONE OF GRACE

**"Therefore let us draw near with confidence
to the throne of grace, so that we may receive
mercy and find grace to help in time of need"
(Hebrews 4:16).**

**"Surely our griefs He Himself bore, and our
sorrows He carried" (Isaiah 53:4).**

Despite my wonderful encounter with our Father's love in Louisville, I found myself in a dramatic battle with grief when I got home. It started with bursting into tears as I pulled onto our property and got worse as I prepared for my first night alone at the farm. The house felt empty and strange without Nicky. All our things were meaningless without him.

I crawled into bed, knowing it was going to be a sleepless and miserable night. In my spirit, I knew I must cling to the incredible experience of God's love given to me as a compass for the days ahead. I must stay focused on Heaven and the eternal realm, but my mind and emotions weren't cooperating. They took me barreling into a world of pain and disorientation I didn't know was possible.

Every level of my soul was in trauma. My mind, my emotions and my body cried out in agony for my husband.[15] Now I knew the fullness of what it meant that Nicky and I were "one" in marriage. In a very real sense, half of me was torn away. All systems were floundering. I was in a surreal world of pain and disorientation I didn't know existed. My mind raced with tormenting thoughts, and everything in me screamed that Nicky should still be with me. But the stark reality was that he was gone. It was final.

In my Christian walk I had never been one to quit or give up. But now I was in so much pain I wasn't sure I could do it anymore. Alarmed by this, I knew I had to overcome the emotional havoc as quickly as possible, so I went to God, seeking Him for answers. I didn't want the opinions or counsel of man. I desperately needed to hear directly from Jesus. I cried out to Him, and He brought two familiar scriptures to my mind: Isaiah 53:4 and Hebrews 4:16.

> "Surely our griefs He Himself bore, and our sorrows He carried..." and "Therefore, let us draw near (come boldly)[16] with confidence to the throne of grace, so that we may receive mercy and find grace to help in time of need."

I cried in a loud voice, "Father, I come to the throne of grace! Lord Jesus, You bore this grief on the cross. I give it to You. Please give me grace!" Thus, I ran to the throne of grace and discovered grief was something I could fight and stop in its tracks when it tried to assail me. When a tidal wave of grief crashed over me, I could resist it and call to Jesus, "I need grace. I need help *now!*" And the ripping emotions would lift off me—until the next assault.

---

[15] I Thess. 5:23. We are a spirit with a soul, living in a body. Our spirits are the deepest part of us. Our souls contain our mind, will, and emotions.

[16] (Come boldly) is from NKJV.

At times, when grief hit so hard that I doubled over in agony, I shouted, "Grace!" as God told Zerubbabel to shout "grace" to the mountain.[17] If I persisted in my resistance to grief, God's grace came each time relieving the pain.

Every moment of my life needed God's grace. As Jesus took me by the hand and led me forward, each step He showed me could only be taken by His grace. He reminded me,

> "I am the vine, you are the branch. . . .apart from
> Me you can do nothing. Cling to Me; don't try
> to rely on your own strength." [18]

It seemed I was whispering, "Help me. Give me grace," with every breath, and this produced a constant dependence on Jesus, sealing me close to His heart in a wonderful way. I came into a higher place with Him than I had known before, and I discovered we have a unique place in His heart as widows. We are a treasured company of women in the kingdom of God as we depend on Him to carry us forward with every step—with every breath.

God's amazing grace became the foundational theme and strength of my walk with Jesus from that day forward. Thus, the title of my book became:

The Widow's Might
Is Found at the Throne of Grace

---

[17] Zech. 4:6, 7
[18] From John 15:5.

PART TWO

WALKING IN GRACE

**"In the beginning was the Word, and the Word
was with God, and the Word was God. And
the Word became flesh, and dwelt among us
. . . full of grace and truth" (John 1:1, 14).**

Jesus is the manifest Word of God. To walk with Him and
know His grace we must fill our hearts with His written Word.
In the following chapters I will share the Scripture verses Jesus
walked me through as He led me into new life. We will pray
as we go. May you have deep encounters with His abounding
love as we walk through the truth of His Word together!

Chapter 1

Encountering Trials

The Testing of Faith

"Consider it all joy, my brethren, when you encounter various trials, knowing that the testing of your faith produces endurance. And let endurance have its perfect result, so that you may be perfect and complete, lacking in nothing" (James 1:2-4).

"No temptation has overtaken you but such as is common to man; and God is faithful, who will not allow you to be tempted beyond what you are able, but with the temptation (test)[19] will provide the way of escape also, so that you will be able to endure it" (1 Corinthians 10:13).

---

[19] Strong's Greek dictionary

*Y*ears ago, during an impossible time in my life, I cried to the Lord, "This is too much. This is wearing me down. I can't take it!" The Holy Spirit corrected me, saying,

> "That's a lie from the devil trying to get you to quit. Trouble is not wearing you down. It's perfecting you. Remember James 1:2-4. Testing produces endurance, and endurance results in you being made perfect and complete—lacking in nothing—so consider what you are going through as joy."

I adjusted my attitude to one of "joy," and James 1:2-4 became a permanent weapon in my arsenal of the Scriptures that took me forward in life. So, while I was reeling in pain after Nicky left for Heaven, I was not surprised when the Lord reminded me of my friend James 1:2-4. I knew it was the truth, and I knew I had a choice to make. I was in the refining fire; my faith was being tested. I could choose to consider what I was going through as "joy" and gain endurance and strength, or I could shrink back and be miserable.

REFINING FIRE

In the kingdom of God, our Father promises to conform us to the image of Christ, and the testing of our faith is part of this process. Just as silver and gold are refined by fire, we are purified as we go through difficult things. God doesn't bring bad things on us, but they happen because there is evil in this fallen world.[20] First Peter 4:12 says, "Beloved, do not be surprised at the fiery ordeal among you, which comes upon you for your testing as though some strange thing were happening to you." Trials, especially fiery ones, are not easy. They

---

[20] Jas. 1:13

shake us to the core. Our flesh recoils from them. Our mind and emotions scream, "No! This can't be happening to me!"

Taking the stance of joy in the face of loss seems impossible to the natural mind. Our souls don't want to consider it anything but tragedy, but this attitude will only take us down instead of up. Choosing joy will strengthen us. I have heard Rick Renner,[21] a notable linguist, say the word, "joy" in James 1:27 should be translated "grace." To me grace and joy go together. God enabling us to do what we cannot do is cause for joy.

First, we must believe God is good, and when He says He will not allow us to go through more than we can bear, we can trust Him. First Corinthians 10:13 says, "No temptation (adversity)[22] has overtaken you but such as is common to man; and God is faithful, who will not allow you to be tempted (tested)[23] beyond what you are able but with the temptation will provide the way of escape also, so that you will be able to endure it."

THE WAY OF ESCAPE

Dealing with grief alone at our farm was too much for me. True to His Word, God made a way of escape for me. He said I must go where He was enthroned on the praises of His people, creating an atmosphere of high-level worship and joy. He told me to move temporarily to Austin, Texas, where celebration before the throne of God goes off the Richter scale at Austin Cathedral. The pastor was a friend of ours. I called him and let him know I was on my way.

In Austin I entered a season of worship and praise—choosing celebration and joy—that kept me focused on Heaven and the fiery encounter with God's love I had experienced in

---

[21] For good Bible study go to https://renner.org/
[22] From Strong's Greek dictionary.
[23] Ibid.

Louisville. I felt His presence in profound ways, and very often I was aware of angels around me. At first, tears were streaming down my cheeks as I struggled to worship, but I was determined to praise Jesus aggressively and joyfully any time the doors were open at the church. It was time to set the course for going forward with God with all my heart. Though I was torn in half and disoriented, I could still *choose* the overcoming attitude of joy. Was I always successful? No. I was on an emotional roller coaster, but I was able to get back up and choose joy each time I hit bottom by praying for grace, and grace kept coming. People saw me as a joyful person, never guessing the hours of prayer it took through sleepless nights to come into that place.

Prayer:

Father, this sounds totally impossible to me as badly as I am hurting. I desperately need Your help if I am to take this attitude of "counting it all joy" in this stage of my life. I have never known such trauma; I am almost crazy with pain. It is beyond description. I come to the throne of grace and ask for help. Help me learn to count it all joy and grow in faith and endurance. Help me! This is impossible without You. Let me feel Your presence and Your wonderful love. I love You, Lord.

STRENGTH

"Do not be grieved, for the joy of the Lord is your strength" (Nehemiah 8:10b).

"A joyful heart is good medicine, But a broken spirit dries up the bones" (Proverbs 17:22).

Nicky had been in Heaven six weeks, and I was visiting family during Christmas. Away from the atmosphere of praise in Austin, I was on the verge of tears as I faced the holidays without him. Then a minister gave me a key to joy. I said, "I am in so much pain, how will I ever have joy again?" Taking my hand, he said, "Come with me," and he took a big leap forward. His demonstration was clear. I had to *decide* to jump into joy. I am so grateful I learned this secret early in my travels as a widow.

It was a simple choice. It didn't mean I *felt* joy, but I chose it; I chose to *act out* joy. Sometimes when I was feeling down, I jumped into joy by deciding to laugh. I still felt torn inside, but I chose to laugh and laughed hard, saying, "Lord, I choose Your joy!" The fact that it seemed so silly released me into real laughter which often turned into laughter from the Lord, and I was refreshed. It is critical to choose joy. Nehemiah tells us the joy of the Lord is our strength. Psalm 17 says, "A joyful heart is good medicine." Choosing joy strengthens our spirits. It is the way of the kingdom of God. Dancing is another way to choose joy. It is my favorite. I turn on the praise music and dance before Jesus, and I am strengthened as His presence comes and His Spirit rises within me.

I would have to remind myself to jump into joy many times as I went forward, especially after leaving the protected atmosphere of praise I enjoyed at Austin Cathedral. Choosing joy became a priority.

Prayer:

Father, my heart is ravaged. I need strength as never before in my life; I need this good medicine of joy You have pre-scribed for me. I take it now, Father—I pray for the grace to choose joy each day—even if it is through sorrow and tears. This is impossible for me except by Your grace, so please help me. Thank You that You are right here as I come before Your throne of grace exalting and worshipping You. Abba, Father, You are worthy of song and celebration! You are the Almighty, my King and my God. You are wonderful!

CHAPTER 2

BE INFORMED ABOUT THOSE WHO SLEEP

TAKE HOPE AND COMFORT

"But we do not want you to be uninformed, brethren, about those who are asleep, *so that you will not grieve as do the rest who have no hope*. For if we believe that Jesus died and rose again, even so God will bring with Him those who have fallen asleep in Jesus. For the Lord Himself will descend from heaven with a shout, with the voice of the archangel and with the trumpet of God, and the dead in Christ will rise first. Then we who are alive and remain will be caught up together with them in the clouds to meet the Lord in the air, and so we shall always be with the Lord. Therefore *comfort one another with these words*" (1 Thessalonians 4:13-18, italics mine).

*A*s I started down the road of life without Nicky, the Lord directed me to 1 Thessalonians 4:13-18. It radiated with the power of the Lord's resurrection and the triumphant hope of His return. Verse 18 said in plain language, "Comfort one another with these words." Yes, comfort is what I had to have, but the Lord offered me much more than comfort. In verse 13 He offered me an escape from grief, saying, "We do not want you to be uninformed, brethren, about those who are asleep, *so that you will not grieve as do the rest who have no hope*" (italics mine).

These verses promised that if I focused on the return of the Lord and the resurrection of the dead I would have hope and be freed from grief. It was a clear offer.

First, it said to be informed about those who had fallen asleep. My husband's remains were laid to rest in the ground but only for a short while. At the Lord's return, in an instant, his body will be resurrected, and his spirit will be reunited with his body. I will join him for eternity, and we will always be together with the Lord. Our separation is temporary, and his body is in the ground momentarily. These words were to comfort me, but how? My emotions were raging within me. Nothing in me wanted any part of this separation. I was in a furious war between my soul and my spirit.

It was one thing to know these verses and another thing to bring them tenaciously into the reality of living them, so they could bring comfort. This was going to take resolve and concerted effort on my part. But how was this any different from taking hold of any of the promises of God? Jesus said in Matthew 11:12, "The kingdom of Heaven suffers violence, and violent men take it by force." It was going to take a fight to apprehend God's solution for me, and it was going to take grace to fight.

The same holds true for you. You can go to God for the grace you need to fight for the comfort He offers us. You will find He is very generous, and He will lavish His grace upon you. He will open His Word to you, and it will become your reality.

Prayer:

Okay, Father, I see what You are saying. I don't want to handle this the wrong way and suffer any more than I am already. I come to Your throne of grace, and I cry out for the help I need to be resolved to search for Your way with all my heart. I pray for grace to come into the reality of the hope of Jesus' return in a fullness that causes the physical world to become dim in the light of Your truth and glory. I want to walk in joy and peace where sorrow and pain don't have a hold on me. I pray for grace, Father, and I receive it. I must have Your grace for it to become real to me that I will be with my husband again soon. I open my heart to You, Holy Spirit. Come with Your power of revelation, and please help me. I receive Your help.

A HOUSE NOT MADE WITH HANDS

"For we know that if the earthly tent which is our house is torn down, we have a building from God, a house not made with hands, eternal in the heavens. For indeed in this house we groan, longing to be clothed with our dwelling from heaven. . . . indeed while we are in this tent, we groan, being burdened, because we do not want to be unclothed but to be clothed, so that what is mortal will be swallowed up by life" (2 Corinthians 5:1, 2, 4).

Paul writes about our physical bodies, calling them our tent or house. We must meditate on this for a moment to realize how temporary this present "housing" is intended to be. It is like inferior clothing that will be taken off and replaced with garments befitting a king. When we put on our dwelling from

Heaven, it is a "rags to riches" story. What is mortal will be swallowed up by life.

Our loved ones are not *swallowed up by death* when they leave us. They are *swallowed up by life* and glad to be shed of the constraints of their mortal bodies. Death, for a child of God, is a day of wonderful liberation.

Those of us who are left behind mourn, but we must also rejoice through our tears. Second Corinthians 5:4 says, "For indeed while we are in this tent, we groan, being burdened, because we do not want to be unclothed, but to be clothed." It is within us to want to live, but it is also within us to long for eternity. Imagine being clothed in garments befitting the royal splendor of Heaven, never to return to the vestments of fallen man. Having been born into this world with bodies which are mere shadows of God's original creation, how wonderful to be free of them at last! To have what is mortal and limiting be swallowed up by what is immortal is the greatest day of our lives.

Home at last in Heaven, we will be steeped in the breath of the living God. Arriving in the heavenly Jerusalem, we will see for ourselves the mysterious realities of Heaven and the majesty of God. We will be able to stand before Him, not to be consumed, but to be wrapped forever in His fiery wonderful love without interruption, completely alive at last!

Prayer:

Abba, Father, help me. While my husband has escaped his temporary tent, You know mine feels as if it has been shredded. This is harder than I could have ever imagined. Give me a taste of Heaven too. I pray, Holy Spirit, come rest on me. I need Your tangible presence.

Father, I pray for the grace to grasp the revelation of what a good and glorious thing it is for my husband to be free at last. Help me put off the mind of man and receive comfort from the mind of Christ. I receive Your grace to rejoice, even through tears, with the comfort of knowing how radiantly happy he is to be with You. I come to Your throne of grace by faith—not seeing it—but my husband beholds all its glory ablaze with mercy. This is amazing! I wonder, Father, does he see me as I come before Your throne? Is he watching? Is he standing there right beside You?

SATISFIED! AWAKE IN HIS LIKENESS

"As for the saints who are in the earth, they are the majestic ones in whom is all my delight. In Your presence is fullness of joy; in Your right hand there are pleasures forever" (Psalm 16:3, 11b).

"I shall behold Your face in righteousness; I will be satisfied with Your likeness when I awake" (Psalm 17:15).

Let's meditate some more on the incredible fact of the coming resurrection of the dead. The Lord said there would be comfort in focusing on this final triumph over death, so let's take time to "drink in" Heaven's perspective on these things.

First, I must say I love the Word of God. Our Father, by His Spirit, can shine His light on His Word one way, and we can see truth. Then He can shine His light from another angle, and like the facets of a gemstone we see another truth shining forth from the same verse. I see this phenomenon in Psalm 16:3,11.

David refers to the saints who are in the earth as the "majestic ones in whom is all his delight." He is writing by the Spirit of God revealing how God sees us. We are delightful to Him. We are majestic before Him. These are wonderful facets of truth, but then it struck me that our loved ones who have gone to Heaven are majestic ones who are "in the earth" in a literal sense. Their bodies rest like hidden treasure in their graves.

In Psalm 17:15 David anticipates beholding God's face and being satisfied with His likeness when he awakes. He longs to awake from the physical life on earth to life in eternity beholding the face of God. Our loved ones are in the presence of God Almighty, and they see His face beaming into theirs. They know pleasure in the fire of His love we can't begin to surround with our imaginations. But there is also great excitement in Heaven as they anticipate "The Day" when the treasure of their bodies will be retrieved from the grave. There is much more glory to come!

All traces of satan's captivity of man will be erased when the Lord Himself returns with a shout, with the voice of the archangel and with the trumpet of God, and the dead in Christ are raised from the grave. In an instant, they will arise as mighty glorious beings in the likeness of the resurrected Christ with immortal, supernatural bodies!

Set your mind on this for a moment. In the beginning God formed Adam out of the dust of the earth and breathed life into him. When Adam sinned, death entered God's perfect creation, and our bodies were doomed to return to the dust of the earth. God didn't like that scenario—He rather liked what He had created. So with salvation through Jesus Christ, He planned not only the saving of our souls, but also the saving of our bodies. He brought man out of the dust of the earth once before, and He is going to do it again. Glory! This event of the resurrection of the "dead in Christ" for the redemption and glorification of our bodies is so grand in the heart of God that He will catch up those who have died out of the grave before catching up those who remain alive on the earth. Think about it! He is delighted with His plan. My wonderful husband is magnificent in Heaven beyond my comprehension, but, oh, what a day is yet to come. Glory to God! Now *that* will be "satisfied—awake in His likeness!"

Prayer:

O Father, I am undone by the wonders of Your great plan of salvation. To know You take such delight in Your creation of man that You have planned the saving of our bodies from the grave is amazing. To know You take delight in me and see me as one of the majestic ones along with those who are in Heaven is wonderful. I soak in the wonder of this tangible hope, that one day we will all be awake in Your likeness. Yes, Father, I drink in Your comfort as I rejoice over my loved one who beholds Your face, satisfied, but with more satisfaction to come. In the fullness of time we will all be raised up and transformed. We will be glorified like Jesus. It won't be said, "From dust to dust" any more. It will be said, "From dust to forever glory!" Thank You, Abba, Father. What a good plan! I like it. When Jesus returns with a shout, what a joyful shout of victory it will be!

CHAPTER 3

LOOK TO HEAVEN

OUR CITIZENSHIP IS IN HEAVEN

"For our citizenship is in heaven, from which also we eagerly wait for a Savior, the Lord Jesus Christ" (Philippians 3:20).

"Therefore, if you have been raised up with Christ, keep seeking the things above, where Christ is, seated at the right hand of God. Set your mind on the things above, not on the things that are on earth" (Colossians 3:1, 2).

After looking to the resurrection of the dead and the return of the Lord to find comfort, the Lord took me to the Scripture verses about Heaven. He said,

"Focus on where Nicky is now instead of where Nicky and you were together in the past. The past is gone. Let go of the past! Your citizenship is in Heaven. Look to your future in eternity."

As I read about Heaven, it became real to me, and I realized why it is so important for us to embrace our new identity when we are born again. We become new creatures in Christ. We are joint heirs with Jesus seated in the heavenly places with Him,[24] and we are to live our lives on earth in eager expectation of what is to come. In Hebrews 11 the Lord points to the example of the great saints of old who said "they were strangers and exiles on the earth," desiring a better country in Heaven where God had prepared a city for them.[25]

Following their example, we are encouraged to consider our lives here as short and temporary even though we are to live to a ripe old age. Colossians 3:2 excites us where it says, "Set your mind on the things above, not on the things that are on earth." Second Corinthians 4:18 says, "Look not at the things which are seen, but at the things which are not seen; for the things which are seen are temporal, but the things which are not seen are eternal."

Jesus said that although we are in the world, we are no longer *of* this world.[26] To overcome the limitations of what we see in the physical world, we must look by the Spirit of God to the invisible city to which we belong. We align our identity and citizenship with Heaven's realities instead of standing earth-bound in our hearts and minds. Hebrews 12:22 says, "You have come to Mount Zion and to the city of the living God." It says, *we have come*—we are there by faith. So let's go! Let's journey into Heaven. Let's fill our minds with the wonders of the eternal where our loved ones who have gone before us rejoice with joy unspeakable. They, at last, see our God in all His glory and the city He has prepared for us.

As we "go to Heaven" through the Scriptures, the Holy Spirit will be our guide. With His help, each narrative will leave us marveling in wonder at the new level of life our loved

---

[24] Eph. 2:6
[25] Heb. 11:13, 14, 16
[26] John 17:16

ones have entered into. Instead of looking back and grieving over what was lost, we can look forward with excitement to where we are going.

First, we will go to the throne of God in Revelation chapter four. It is one of the most brilliant descriptions of Heaven found in Scripture. John is on the Isle of Patmos, living in exile, when God says, "Come up here." He is caught up to the throne of the Almighty, his senses taking in grandeur, splendor and majesty which defy human imagination. Before we join him let's pray.

Prayer:

Heavenly Father, I don't want to read about these marvels in the dullness of my mind and limited intellect. I don't want to lean on my own understanding.[27] I want the Holy Spirit to quicken me to the realities of the kingdom of Heaven. Help me, by grace, to be thrilled with Your glory and be encouraged. I pray for an encounter with Your living Word that delights me with the joy of Heaven and carries me away from grief. I pray You will help me come alive in my heart to Your majesty and glory. Yes, Father, I want to "come up," like John. Thank You for Your help.

"Come Up Here"—Revelation 4:1-11

After these things I looked, and behold, a door standing open in heaven, and the first voice which I had heard, like the sound of a trumpet speaking with me, said, "Come up here, and I will show you what must take place after these things." Immediately I was in the Spirit; and behold, a throne was standing in heaven, and One sitting on the throne (verses 1, 2).

---

[27] Prov. 3:5

And He Who sat there appeared like [the crystalline brightness of] jasper and [the fiery] sardius, and encircling the throne there was a halo that looked like [a rainbow of] emerald (verse 3, AMPC).

Around the throne were twenty-four thrones; and upon the thrones I saw twenty-four elders sitting, clothed in white garments, and golden crowns on their heads. Out from the throne came flashes of lightning and sounds and peals of thunder. And there were seven lamps of fire burning before the throne, which are the seven Spirits of God (verses 4, 5).

And before the throne there was something like a sea of glass, like crystal; and in the center and around the throne, four living creatures full of eyes in front and behind. The first creature was like a lion, and the second creature like a calf, and the third creature had a face like that of a man, and the fourth creature was like a flying eagle (verses 6, 7).

And the four living creatures, each one of them having six wings, are full of eyes around and within; and day and night they do not cease to say, "HOLY, HOLY, HOLY IS THE LORD GOD, THE ALMIGHTY, WHO WAS AND WHO IS AND WHO IS TO COME" (verse 8).

And when the living creatures give glory and honor and thanks to Him who sits on the throne, to Him who lives forever and ever, the twenty-four elders will fall down before Him who sits on the throne, and will worship Him who lives forever and ever, and will cast their crowns before the throne, saying, "Worthy are You, our Lord and our God, to receive glory and honor and power; for You created all things, and because of Your will they existed, and were created" (verses 9-11).

Prayer:

Father, illuminate my imagination, for I want to take a deep drink from what I am reading. What do you mean by a voice that sounds like a trumpet? It must have been loud and clarion and supernatural. Your appearance is like a jasper stone, which is a crystal-clear[28] gemstone, and like a sardius stone which is red, and You say that I am made in Your image? Is it that Your appearance is crystal clear, but also glowing like fire and brilliantly shining, yet with the form of a man? Why is there an emerald rainbow around Your throne? Is it Your force of life radiating from You and Your brilliance? Who are the twenty-four elders seated on thrones encircling Your throne? You don't tell us clearly in Your Word. Why do You keep their identity a mystery? Ha! You enjoy mystery!

What is this "something like a sea of glass" that is like crystal? Glass and crystal are solid, but You call it a sea. Is it amazingly clear water unlike anything on earth that is both solid and liquid? In Revelation 15 the sea of glass is mixed with fire, and people are standing there holding harps. In other places You talk about the river of life coming from Your throne.

The seven Spirits of God are seven lamps of fire burning before Your throne. Now what a vibrant living blaze this must be, along with the flashes of lightning!

You say there are lightning flashes and sounds and peals of thunder. It must be glorious and awesome to hear Heaven. I can't imagine the resonance of "the sounds" and peals of thunder mixed with the shouts and songs of praise that are continuous around Your throne. Father, what are the sounds that accompany the peals of thunder? John only calls them sounds.

Father, why did You create the four living creatures full of eyes, with wings, and eyes even in the wings? They sound bizarre to me, but they must be wonderful if You stand them

---

[28] Rev. 21:11

before Your throne. There is nothing like them on earth. Amazing! It blesses me to think my sweet husband sees these indescribable wonders. O Father, I must rise up out of grief and rejoice with him as he stands in full awe of You at last. I know he is crying out with the living creatures, "HOLY, HOLY, HOLY IS THE LORD GOD, THE ALMIGHTY, WHO WAS AND WHO IS AND WHO IS TO COME."

Yes, Father, I cry out too, "HOLY, HOLY, HOLY IS THE LORD GOD, THE ALMIGHTY, WHO WAS AND WHO IS AND WHO IS TO COME." I worship You, Almighty God, my Abba, Father. I love You.

LIGHT, LIGHT, LIGHT

"Every perfect gift is from above, coming down from the Father of lights, with whom there is no variation or shifting shadow" (James 1:17).

"You are clothed with splendor and majesty, covering Yourself with light as with a cloak, stretching out heaven like a tent curtain" (Psalm 104:1b, 2).

"He who is the blessed and only Sovereign, the King of kings and Lord of lords, who alone possesses immortality and *dwells in unapproachable light*, whom no man has seen or can see. To Him be honor and eternal dominion!" (1 Timothy 6:15, 16, italics mine).

"And the city has no need of the sun or of the moon to shine on it, for the glory of God has illumined it, and its lamp is the Lamb" (Revelation 21:23).

In Heaven God is the source of all light, and there are no shadows. Amazing! Friends, we must be delivered from our propensity to read amazing things in the Word of God but miss their magnitude. God our Father is referred to as "the Father of lights, with whom there is no variation or shifting shadow" (James 1:17). How many times have we read this verse without meditating on God being the "Father of Lights"? Think of it! If it were not for God, there would be no light. Certainly there would be no life or revelation and guidance from God as well, but consider first: there would be no light.

God is "clothed with splendor and majesty, covering Himself with light as with a cloak, stretching out heaven like a tent curtain" (Psalm 104:1b, 2). Our Father clothes Himself with light! To Him, the universe is just a curtain He has stretched out to display the sun, moon and stars in its expanse. Our own sun is but a small flicker in comparison to the magnificent blaze of giant stars our Father has hung in space; yet we can't bear to look directly into its light. If the brilliance of our own sun is blinding, how much more blinding is it to look upon almighty God who is the source of all light?

First Timothy 6:16 reveals that this light is unapproachable. The book of Revelation tells us the heavenly Jerusalem "has no need of the sun or of the moon to shine on it, for the glory of God has illumined it, and its lamp is the Lamb. . . . There will no longer be any night; and they will not have need of the light of a lamp nor the light of the sun, because the Lord God will illumine them" (Rev. 21:23; 22:5).

Think of the brilliance and glory of God, the Father of lights, and yet, through the blood of Jesus, we are made acceptable to Him as though we never sinned. Because of Jesus, those who have preceded us into His full glory are able to stand before Him without being consumed. They stand and live eternally in the radiance of His unapproachable light.

Prayer:

O wonderful Father, I have no choice but to agree wholeheartedly with Your Word that says we must "show gratitude, by which we may offer to You an acceptable service with reverence and awe; for You our God are a consuming fire" (see Heb. 12:28, 29). Yes! I thank You, Father, for this great salvation through the blood of Jesus Christ. I thank You for creating me. I stand in awe of You. Thank You for creating me to be in eternity with You forever. The thought that I will dwell in Your unapproachable light overwhelms my small imagination. I worship You and magnify You. Give me grace to be embossed with gratitude! Engrave upon my heart the thanksgiving due to You, my awesome Father and God, who gathers me to Yourself as Your child. Amazing. It is amazing that You invite me to call You, "Abba! Father!"[29] I worship You and hunger for more of You. I am thrilled at the day approaching when I too will step into Your unapproachable light.

THE PAVEMENT OF SAPPHIRE

"Then Moses went up the mountain with Aaron, Nadab and Abihu, and seventy of the elders of Israel, and they saw the God of Israel; and under His feet there appeared to be a pavement of sapphire, as clear as the sky itself. Yet He did not stretch out His hand against the nobles of the sons of Israel; and they saw God, and they ate and drank" (Exodus 24:9-11).

In the book of Exodus, Moses, Aaron, Nadab, Abihu and seventy of the elders of Israel peer into the supernatural realm of eternity at the same time. They see God, and they eat and drink in His presence. You'd think a lot would have been written about this. Of all the things that could have been said we are told only where God stood. It says, "Under His feet there appeared to be a pavement of sapphire, as clear as the sky itself." For some reason, in this glimpse of God, He wants us

---

[29] Rom. 8:15, Gal. 4:6

42

to know there is a pavement like sapphire in Heaven. Will we walk there as well as on the streets of gold? I don't know about you, but my thoughts race with questions. Can you imagine if you were among those left in the camp below? I can hear the wives of the seventy elders asking questions late into the night when their husbands returned from the mountain.

I think our wonderful Father smiles at this. He is whetting our appetites as His children, building our excitement for big surprises. He is hinting at wonders beyond description in a place far superior to the physical confines of earth. While we stand with our feet planted on earth, we are invited to consider where He stands. We have a marvelous destination, and when we get there we will be saying, "Oh, this is what they saw!"

Until then, like children, we are to be eager and hopeful, looking forward to the day when we will break through into the glory of Heaven. Our loved ones who are there will surround us with laughter. They will be excited to see us and our amazement as eternity bursts forth in unveiled splendor before our eyes. Like little children with the blindfolds finally removed, we will at last see the surprises our Father has been hinting at in His Word. What a "Welcome Home" celebration filled with surprise and wonder awaits us!

Prayer:

O Father! Wonderful Abba, Father, am I to laugh or cry? The anticipation is too much for me. Keep me mindful of Heaven, and help me never forget the great day that is ahead of me. Rejoicing in hope is a good word for it. Is that what is stirring in my heart? As I sit here so excited in my heart, does my loved one look in on me? Who is watching from the cloud of witnesses? Angels? My parents? My husband? Are You looking down on me, Father? Hallelujah! I join the worship of Heaven—I worship You, Father.

EZEKIEL'S FOUR CREATURES

"As I looked, behold, a storm wind was coming from the north, a great cloud with fire flashing forth continually and a bright light around it, and in its midst something like glowing metal in the midst of the fire. Within it there were figures resembling four living beings. And this was their appearance: they had human form. Each of them had four faces and four wings. Their legs were straight and their feet were like a calf's hoof, and they gleamed like burnished bronze. Under the wings on their four sides were human hands. As for the faces and wings of the four of them, their wings touched one another; their faces did not turn when they moved, each went straight forward. . . ; each had the face of a man; all four had the face of a lion on the right and the face of a bull on the left, and all four had the face of an eagle. . . . And each went straight forward; wherever the spirit was about to go, they would go, without turning as they went" (Ezekiel 1:4-10,12).

In the book of Ezekiel, the prophet describes God coming to have a talk with him. It takes him twenty-eight verses to describe God's approach, and so great and terrible in power and amazement is the vision that Ezekiel falls on his face trembling. I encourage you to read the whole chapter and be amazed at the wonder and power of our supernatural God. Ezekiel says the heaven opened and he saw a storm wind approaching, with a great cloud and fire flashing forth. A bright light surrounded it, and something like glowing metal was inside. Within all this he sees four creatures. The configuration seems to be a living vehicle, for it all moved wherever the Spirit was about to go with wheels and eyes on the wheels.[30] The four creatures are in and of this vehicle or supernatural storm above which Ezekiel sees a throne. The prophet

---

[30] Ezek. 1:15-18

struggles to describe that which is too fantastic and unlike our world to describe.

Is this what it looks like when God decides to ride upon the clouds?[31] Is this His chariot? In these passages we are being given much to ignite our imaginations as we marvel and wonder about the invisible dimensions of Heaven.

The four creatures described here are different from the four creatures that stand around the throne in Revelation 4. These creatures have four wings instead of six. Their faces are like the faces of the four creatures in Revelation 4, but they have four faces each. These four-faced creatures move without turning, as the Spirit of God moves.

How many creatures has God made with these faces? The face of the man, the lion, the bull and the eagle. Will Heaven be filled with this imagery?

Scholars have a lot to say about all this, but we don't have to understand it all to be brought forth in amazement by reading these verses.[32] Considering the unseen realms of eternity, we can marvel at our God and that we are His. We can let our hearts be filled with worship as we look to our certain destination as citizens of Heaven.

Prayer:

Wonderful Father, thank You for this description of what can't be described! Thank You for prodding my imagination and heart with stirrings from Heaven so that I am left wondering and amazed. One day I will actually see Your chariot and these four living beings and say, "Oh, so *this* is what Ezekiel saw!" Help me, Father, to be in a constant state of awe and anticipation of the wonders that will unfold for me in eternity. Help me stay in awe and wonder, longing to see

---

[31] Ps. 104:3

[32] I recommend Louada Raschke's "Face the Whirlwind" at www.louada.org.

You and all You have made beyond the restrictions of earth and time. I love You.

ISAIAH SEES THE LORD

"In the year of King Uzziah's death I saw the Lord sitting on a throne, lofty and exalted, with the train of His robe filling the temple. Seraphim stood above Him, each having six wings: with two he covered his face, and with two he covered his feet, and with two he flew. And one called out to another and said, 'Holy, Holy, Holy is the Lord of hosts; the whole earth is full of His glory.' And the foundations of the thresholds trembled at the voice of him who called out, while the temple was filling with smoke. Then I said, 'Woe is me, for I am ruined! Because I am a man of unclean lips ... For my eyes have seen the King, the Lord of hosts'" (Isaiah 6:1-5).

Isaiah 6 gives us a profound picture of the eternal things that are hidden from our sight. The prophet is taken into a vision where he sees the Lord on His throne in the temple. There is no mention of the river flowing from the throne, the sea of glass or the four living creatures. In this moment, all attention is on the Lord of hosts magnifying His majesty and glory. Can we begin to imagine the splendid royal robe He is wearing? The train fills the entire temple of Heaven. Where is there such a king on earth? God is the divine King with whom no earthly king can compare!

The seraphim cover their faces with their wings—their countenance is not to be seen—not to be compared to the great Lord of hosts. Yet so mighty are the seraphim that the threshold trembles as one seraphim calls out in his great voice, "Holy, holy, holy is the Lord of hosts; the whole earth is full of His glory." What a beautiful, powerful, resounding cry as smoke fills the temple and the foundations shake! Yes, indeed, the full attention of this holy vision is on the magnificence of our God as He is declared the holy Lord of hosts. He is the Lord of every entity, of the entire angelic host and all His created beings. There is nothing to which He is not the Lord. Overwhelmed by the vision, Isaiah fears for his life, saying, "Woe is me, for I am ruined! Because I am a man of unclean lips. . . . For my eyes have seen the King, the Lord of hosts" (Isa. 6:5).

One day, we too will see our God upon His throne, and because of the blood of Jesus, we will not perish in His presence. Instead we will bow before Him, joining the voices of the seraphim crying, "Holy, holy, holy is the Lord of hosts. The whole earth is full of His glory. Holy, holy, holy is the Lord of hosts!" The day is fast approaching when every knee will bow and every tongue will confess that Jesus Christ is Lord. We will see Him as Isaiah saw Him, but with the power of eternity completely unveiled.

Prayer:

Wonderful God, why should I wait until I am in Heaven to extol You, Lord of hosts? Father, I join with the seraphim now. Now I cry out, "Holy, holy, holy is the Lord of hosts. The whole earth is full of Your glory." Now I exalt You and lend my voice to magnify and glorify You. Now I worship You. How I yearn for the day when I will be there in fullest measure to behold You on Your throne. I love You, my mighty God and my King! Father, I would like to have visions of Heaven like so many of Your servants in the Bible. That would be wonderful. Please open my eyes to dreams and visions. Yes, Lord, I would like to have visions.

WE HAVE COME TO MOUNT ZION

"But you have come to Mount Zion and to the city of the living God, the heavenly Jerusalem, and to myriads of

angels, to the general assembly and church of the first-born who are enrolled in heaven, and to God, the Judge of all, and to the spirits of the righteous made perfect and to Jesus, the mediator of a new covenant, and to the sprinkled blood, which speaks better than the blood of Abel" (Hebrews 12:22-24).

"For now we see in a mirror dimly, but then face to face; now I know in part, but then I will know fully just as I also have been fully known" (1 Corinthians 13:12).

Hebrews 12:22-24 tells us we have come "to Mount Zion and to the city of the living God, the heavenly Jerusalem." It doesn't say we are going to get there later. It says we have come. Although we are on earth in physical bodies, we are also in heavenly places in our spirit. This is a wonderful mystery in the kingdom of God. Our loved ones who have gone before us are there, and we are there with them. Verses 22 and 23 say we have come "to myriads of angels, to the general assembly and church of the firstborn who are enrolled in Heaven, and to God, the Judge of all, and to the spirits of the righteous made perfect."

The "church of the firstborn who are enrolled in Heaven" describes the Christians, here on earth, whose names are recorded in the Lamb's book of life. We are right there with the spirits of the righteous made perfect, the Christians who have died and gone to Heaven. Ha! Their bodies may have died, but they are vibrantly alive. They are more alive than we can comprehend, and we have all come to Jesus. They are connected to Jesus, and we are connected to Jesus. They see the glories of Heaven clearly, but we who are here on earth "see in a mirror dimly" (1 Cor. 13:12). They see Jesus face-to-face now, and we will see Him face-to-face too when we leave our bodies as they have.

Embracing this truth through the help of the Holy Spirit brings us away from the loss of those who have fallen asleep. We can't see them, but they are right there, just as Jesus is right there. They are in Him, and we are in Him. This is a wonderful supernatural mystery. Anticipation supersedes grief; awareness that we are not far removed from each other, just in different dimensions, gives a whole new definition to our temporary separation. It is as though we are still in the same house together, but they are in another room. We are in Christ, and they are in Christ; but they are in another and much brighter room, and we can rejoice for them. We must! As the reality of this great wonder floods our hearts, there is a place for joy. It is a joy that transforms our tears and calms our raging emotions as we partake of this certainty and wonder of the kingdom of Heaven. We are drawn into worship, which is the very atmosphere of Heaven. We breathe the air of worship with longings too deep for words.

Prayer:

Abba, Father, this sounds good to me, and I want to come into this place of deep worship and comfort. I must come. I need these tears to be transformed into tears of joy and antic-ipation instead of tears of sorrow. Holy Spirit, please help me know this nearness of my loved one. Help me "breathe in" this atmosphere of the glory of God. Make it real to me, I pray. Help my aching heart transcend into glorious worship in a way I have never known before. I pray for Your grace and thank You for it.

THE HEAVENLY JERUSALEM

"And he. . .showed me the holy city, Jerusalem. . .having the glory of God. Her brilliance was like a very costly stone, as a stone of crystal-clear jasper.

It had a great and high wall, with twelve gates, and at the gates twelve angels; and names were written on them, which are the names of the twelve tribes of the sons of Israel. There were three gates on the east and three gates on the north and three gates on the south and three gates on the west.

And the wall of the city had twelve foundation stones, and on them were the twelve names of the twelve apostles of the Lamb. . . .The city is laid out as a square, and its length is as great as the width. . .fifteen hundred miles; its length and width and height are equal.

And he measured its wall, seventy-two yards, according to human measurements, which are also angelic measurements. The material of the wall was jasper; and the city was pure gold, like clear glass.

The foundation stones of the city wall were adorned with every kind of precious stone. The first foundation stone was jasper; the second, sapphire; the third, chalcedony; the fourth, emerald; the fifth, sardonyx; the sixth, sardius; the seventh, chrysolite; the eighth, beryl; the ninth, topaz; the tenth, chrysoprase; the eleventh, jacinth; the twelfth, amethyst.

And the twelve gates were twelve pearls; each one of the gates was a single pearl. And the street of the city was pure gold, like transparent glass. . . .And the city has no need of the sun or of the moon to shine on it, for the glory of God has illumined it, and its lamp is the Lamb" (Revelation 21:10-23).

Read this description of our city over and over again. It sparkles and radiates with more intensity, vibrant living color, and wonderment each time we take it into our spirits. What glorious beauty! We will be astonished to actually walk its "clear like glass" streets of pure gold. Pure gold by Heaven's standard is clear—and we will walk there! The walls are of crystal clear jasper mounted on twelve strata of enormous brilliant gemstones laid as her foundation. Their display of multiple and various colors dance with the glory of the light of God beaming through their many facets. And Jerusalem's dimensions, why, they leave us speechless. Fifteen hundred miles would be half the distance across the United States, and she is as high as she is long! Her walls are 216 feet. What colossal pearl gates she must host! Imagine, which we can't, the magnificence and stature of the angels guarding each of the twelve gates. Are they robed in glorious gemstone colors with ornaments of gold to complement the foundation stones, or are they robed in white? Certainly, they are filled with exploding joy! Are my imaginings accurate? We will see! Yes, we *will* see, and that is the sheer glory of the hope and destiny we hold in Christ.

Prayer:

O Father, there aren't words to express what burns in my heart for what awaits us in our city, the heavenly Jerusalem. Inscribe upon my heart this anticipation, so that it never leaves me. Burn it deep into my soul so that it is carried with me like a compass in my heart, forever drawing me to my home with You. Cause it to shine and radiate in my imagination and draw me closer, ascending evermore in my heart, longing and gazing toward Heaven. Yes, Jesus, in Your name I pray and wait for You.

CHAPTER 4

THE RELUCTANT BRIDE

**"Hallelujah! For the Lord our God, the
Almighty, reigns. Let us rejoice and be glad
and give the glory to Him, for the marriage of
the Lamb has come and His bride has made
herself ready" (Revelation 19:6b, 7).**

In the Bible the imagery of our being the bride of Christ
is clear. This is seen in Ephesians where the marriage
between a man and a woman is compared to the relationship we have with the Lord.[33] We are His bride, and He is our
Bridegroom. Mankind was created by his Creator to be mar-
velously joined with Him as one.[34]

I knew Jesus as my Bridegroom and first love while Nicky
and I were married, and the love we shared was wonderful
because Jesus was in the middle of it. But now that Nicky was
living in Heaven, it was time to let go of him and rededicate
myself completely to Jesus. I needed to say, "Yes," to Him as

---

[33] Eph. 5:22
[34] See John 17:21.

His bride and make myself ready for the day when the bride will join the Bridegroom at the marriage of the Lamb.

SHIFTING GEARS

I knew, in my head, that I must take Jesus as my husband. But what my head was saying and what my heart was saying were two different things. Everything in me wanted Nicky back. A real war was going on inside me. I was worshipping Jesus, clinging to Him and trying to walk in joy, but my heart was not completely His. I was in a serious struggle I had to work through. I resented the title "widow." Everything about me was geared for marriage and being a helpmate to my husband. I had to shift gears, but the clutch wasn't working. It was grinding!

A dear widow said, "You have a wonderful identity to step into in this new season of your life." I didn't like hearing that. It didn't sound wonderful to me. It sounded like a prison sentence. My husband had left for Heaven much sooner than I could have imagined, and my emotions were in full rebellion to my new place in life. I wanted to scream, "I'm not a widow!" But of course I was.

I was still so attached to Nicky that when I went to Heaven I wanted to see him before seeing anyone else, and that included Jesus. A friend said, "You need to let go of Nicky," and he was right. I am being candid here because many are reacting the same way I did, and it is liberating to know that others have felt the same way. We are not condemned. Jesus will bring us through it.

LOOKING BACKWARD AND FORWARD

I had difficulty with looking backward and difficulty with looking forward. The past was over and gone—to go there was painful. It only magnified the fact that our wonderful life together had been taken from me and made me cry all the more.

Looking forward held anxiety and fear. Struggling with the confusion and memory loss that came with the trauma I was in was frightening. I couldn't remember half of what was said to me. How was I going to navigate life in this condition?

The Lord kept steering me to the present where each day had enough trouble of its own.[35] He called me to take His arm as His bride and trust and depend on Him one step at a time, one moment at a time. He kept saying, "Don't look back," reminding me that "no one, after putting his hand to the plow and looking back, is fit for the kingdom of God" (Luke 9:62).

Being able to keep my mind on the present and not look back was not an overnight victory for me. I was flooded with thoughts of my life with Nicky. So I put away the pictures and things that stirred memories of the past. To keep my mind focused, I placed a wonderful picture of Nicky when he was twenty-four on my dresser. This is how I believe he looks now and how he will greet me when I go to Heaven. He is young and handsome and at the peak of health.[36]

LOOKING FORWARD

Looking too far forward, instead of concentrating on one day at a time, held a different pitfall. I was flooded with thoughts of being married again. The fantasy of meeting a new husband came at me relentlessly, playing on a desire to be rescued—to be held. Most of my older friends didn't have any desire for a new husband. But I knew others who had remarried quickly and were met with disaster. Their stories were a warning to me. This was a season in which I needed to

---

[35] Matt. 6:34
[36] Ps. 103:5

learn contentment with God in my new circumstances instead of looking for an escape.[37]

People unwittingly said, "Oh, you are so young! Don't you want to be married again?" Their comments bothered me. As I wrestled with this, another widow said, "Margie, in your book please tell people to stop asking widows if they want to remarry." I thought, *Oh, so you've heard this one too!*

I'm just sharing honestly with you. Someone out there needs to know the way they are processing their loss and the things that are coming at them are common patterns for widows. Jesus will guide you through it. It is important to be honest with God about your struggles in every way. After all He knows all your thoughts and the secrets of your heart better than you do. I confessed these attitudes and emotions to Jesus as they came up and prayed for the grace to get past them. I didn't lose sight of my goal as a Christian to be an overcomer, but I had to deal with things hidden in my heart. One by one the Lord was bringing them to the surface.

THE OLD CYCLE

Part of my struggle was the cycles and routines of life my husband and I had shared. For example, I was in the habit of fixing Nicky's meals and shopping for the two of us according to his likes and dislikes. Suddenly all of that was gone, and a trip to buy groceries was now foreign territory.

I felt a terrible emptiness shopping for one and planning meals just for myself. The grocery store became a battlefield of grief. I had to walk carefully to control my emotions, crying out under my breath for grace to make it through the store without bursting into tears. I would gather up only what was necessary and leave as quickly as I could.

---

[37] Phil. 4:11, AMPC

Finally, I went on the offensive and took the grocery store on as a mission field. I still had a lump in my throat, but I looked for widows to encourage or someone who looked lonely and made a point of being friendly to them. I discovered the grocery store was full of lonely people.

Handling the finances, maintenance for the car, getting dressed and going somewhere, even doing the laundry—you name it, every process of life was missing Nicky, and everywhere he was missing, it hurt.

Now in all these things I leaned on Jesus and prayed for grace and was in continual conversation with Him. I desperately had to have Jesus. I needed His help at every turn. If I couldn't find my glasses or my keys, I would ask for His help just as I used to ask Nicky for help. I would push down the panic and say, "Jesus, please set my eyes on my keys," and before long I would find them. All the while, however, this was accompanied with an ache in my heart; it had always been my husband's role to find my keys and my glasses when we were going somewhere. He was so patient and even amused that I never knew where they were. So you see, every time I had to call on Jesus, it was also a reminder of my loss. I wanted Nicky instead of Jesus.

KICKING AGAINST THE GOADS

I must confess I was hesitant to take Jesus completely as my husband because I was tempted in my heart to resent God for my new circumstances. *I knew better than to be angry with Him*, but my heart was hanging back. Oh, to be honest, it was a stance of "I hate what has happened to me!" One friend of mine put it another way when her husband died. She cried out, "I hate my life with John gone!"

I think this is what it means in the book of Acts where it says, "It is hard for you to kick against the goads" (Acts 26:14b). In my heart I was kicking.

It was obviously time to move forward with Jesus, and I didn't want to—but I had to. I needed Jesus as my husband, but I didn't want Him. I leaned on Jesus, but I didn't like it. What a rotten place I had discovered in my heart! Of course, I took all of this to confession and prayer. "Jesus, I confess I don't want You as my husband. This is awful. I see what is in my heart. I'm being exposed. Lord, forgive me. Help me!"

FINALLY A BRIDE

One day a minister spoke by the Holy Spirit and said, "The day will come when you will be excited to lay your head on your pillow at night because Jesus will be there." He didn't know I was widowed. He didn't know the hardest time for me was going to bed at night without Nicky, but Jesus knew.

I was reminded again and again of what he had said until the day came when I finally said, "Okay, Lord. I don't want to wish Nicky were here anymore, and I don't want to wish I were married again. I just want You. All these desires have been hurting me instead of helping me. Forgive me and help me." I would crawl into bed and lay my head down and say, "Now where are You, Jesus? Please talk to me and hold me." I chose to believe He was there even if all was silent. I chose to believe He was holding me even if I didn't feel a thing. "Jesus, it is You and me."

At last, I was committed. It was easier to stop drifting into memories, and the sense of loss started to fade and become more distant. Now I was longing for Jesus instead of Nicky. Looking to the future amounted to trusting Jesus that it would be good. He would walk me through it one day at a time.

It was Jesus who brought me to this place of full surrender to Him. I couldn't have done it by myself. My responsibility was to confess my weakness and ask for grace as He showed me what was in my heart. It was His job to pour His grace on me and get me through, and He did.

THERE IS NO CONDEMNATION

I am impressed by God's amazing love and patience with me. As my husband, Jesus was married to someone who didn't really want Him, was using Him and was longing for someone else. Yet He kept standing with me in every way I would let Him until I was able to shift gears.

Now you know what? I am not condemned by this. What I was going through is common for the human heart dealing with the loss of a great love. You don't spin on a dime in the transition. I had asked Jesus to do a quick work in me, and I think that is what He did. Of course I know there is more work to be done until I have finished my race, but I have great confidence that He will be faithful to me. There is no chance of betrayal. His love is unfailing.

RADIANT BRIDE

I have accepted the title of "widow," but that sounds as if I am without a husband. I prefer the title of "bride." Jesus is my Husband. I am His bride. I have stood before the mirror and said, "Lord, make me radiant. I want to glow with You. I want to look like someone who is in love with her Bridegroom." The image that looks back at me is not always so sunny, but the progress is unmistakable. He is doing it. I have prayed Psalm 34:5. It says, "They looked to Him and were radiant, and their faces will never be ashamed." I am expecting to become radiant because I have taken this to the throne of grace. Jesus will bring it to pass.

The following chapter is taken from my times of final surrender to Jesus as my Bridegroom as He poured His love on me. As you read, enter into free conversation with Jesus knowing that nothing in your heart is hidden from Him. He offers a love beyond your imagination. There is great healing for you in His love. Take the time to read slowly and let the living Word become part of you. I have personalized Paul's prayer from Ephesians 3:14-20 so you can pray it as you prepare to walk down the aisle into the arms of Jesus as your Bridegroom.

Prayer:

Father, I want to say, "Yes," to Jesus. I want to get past the struggles of identity from having been a wife to my husband and take Jesus as my Bridegroom. I bow before You, asking You to please grant me, according to the riches of Your glory, to be strengthened with power through Your Spirit in the inner man. I want Jesus to dwell in my heart through faith. I want to be rooted and grounded in His love, comprehending and knowing the love of Christ which surpasses knowledge. Fill me up to all the fullness of God. Yes, I ask for Your wonderful grace to help me open my heart completely to Jesus.

CHAPTER 5

THE BRIDE AND THE BRIDEGROOM

THE BRIDEGROOM HOLDS THE BRIDE

"'I am not the Christ, but I have been sent ahead of Him.' "He who has the bride is the bridegroom; but the friend of the bridegroom, who stands and hears him, rejoices greatly because of the bridegroom's voice" (John 3:28, 29).

"I give eternal life to them, and they will never perish; and no one will snatch them out of My hand. My Father, who has given them to Me, is greater than all; and no one is able to snatch them out of the Father's hand" (John 10:28, 29).

This is amazing. In John 3:28, John the Baptist identifies Jesus as the Bridegroom. He rejoices as he reveals the relationship of the church to the Savior. She is the bride, and

Jesus, the Son of God, is the Bridegroom. What an unexpected pronouncement to those looking for the Savior, the Messiah. But look closely:

He says, "He who *has the bride* is the bridegroom." Wonderful bride of Christ—Jesus—your Husband has you. This is astonishing. He has you.

In John 10:28, 29 Jesus says of His bride, "I give eternal life to them, and they will never perish; and no one will snatch them out of My hand. My Father, who has given them to Me, is greater than all; and no one is able to snatch them out of the Father's hand."

This is wonderful. The Father and the Son who are one hold the bride securely in their hands. Rejoice, O bride of Christ! You can't be snatched away by any evil or calamity, for our God who spread out the heavens with His right hand holds you in that same hand.

Let your eyes feast on these next verses. Let them take hold in your heart:

"Surely My hand founded the earth, and My right hand spread out the heavens. . ." (Isa. 48:13). "Do not fear, for I am with you; do not anxiously look about you, for I am your God. I will strengthen you, surely I will help you, surely I will uphold you with My righteous right hand" (Isa. 41:10).

Paul further exalts our God's all-powerful hold on us in Romans 8:38, 39. "For I am convinced that neither death, nor life, nor angels, nor principalities, nor things present, nor things to come, nor powers, nor height, nor depth, nor any other created thing, will be able to separate us from the love of God, which is in Christ Jesus our Lord."

What a marriage we enjoy with our adoring Bridegroom! He assures us we are safe. We are His treasured bride to whom He says, "Do not fear, for I am with you. Surely I will uphold you." O Bride, we are held in the hand of our Bridegroom. Nothing can withstand His love for us!

Prayer:

Father, I come running to Your throne of grace! I say, "Yes, I take Jesus as my Savior, as my Husband." Abba, Father, give me the grace to so embrace Jesus as my Bridegroom in the secret place, that all trace of fear is driven from my heart to never rise again. I will say, "You have enclosed me behind, and before and laid Your hand upon me. Such knowledge is too wonderful for me" (Psalm 139:5, 6a). May I be among those in whom perfect love has cast out all fear![38] Father, I want to be found trusting You and praising You no matter what comes upon this earth. Give me grace not to neglect so great a salvation. Keep me from the mires of religion. Drench me in the dew of Heaven, watering my soul with grace. O Father, You will do it! You will pour Your grace upon me, and I will know the perfect love of the Bridegroom. I will not neglect Him. I will be convinced of His love no matter what arises before me. I give my life to Him. Thank You, Father.

THE BRIDE PREPARES HERSELF

"Let us rejoice and shout for joy. . . . The marriage of the Lamb has come, and His bride has prepared herself. She has been permitted to dress in fine (radiant) linen, dazzling and white—for the fine linen (represents) the righteousness, (and godly living, and right standing with God) of (God's holy people). . . .Blessed are those who are invited to the marriage supper of the Lamb" (Revelation 19:7-9b).[39]

"The bridegroom came, and those who were ready went in with him to the wedding feast; and the door was shut.

---

[38] See 1 John 4:18.
[39] Adapted from AMPC.

Later the other virgins also came, saying, 'Lord, lord, open up for us.' But he answered, 'Truly I say to you, I do not know you'" (Matthew 25:10b-12).

Revelation 19 speaks of the great day when the bride of Christ sits down at the marriage supper of the Lamb. The bride looks forward to this and makes herself ready. She is already betrothed to Jesus as her Husband while on earth, but there is the great event of arriving in Heaven. Then, when all the members of the bride arrive at the end of the age, the wedding feast will take place.

We all know our life on earth will come to an end one day, but acknowledgement of our mortality is not enough to make us get ready. It is God's revelation of the Bridegroom and our love for Him that spawn preparation. To the bride, His coming for her is not a distant event to prepare for later. Her heartbeat is in a rhythm of desire to have her Husband now. He is her priority.

There is no possibility she will be turned away from the wedding feast with the Bridegroom saying, "I don't know you" (Matt. 25:12). She won't be among those who were not ready and to whom the door was shut. The bride and the Bridegroom know each other, and her desire for Him has birthed hours of drawing aside with Him. She is seen at the throne of grace daily where she cries out to walk in His likeness. Everything that comes to light in her that is not pleasing to Him is something she must be rid of. Her desire is to be holy because He is holy.This is her motivation. She clothes herself in fine linen by repenting, confessing her sins and being washed by the blood of the Lamb in a continual walk with Jesus. She doesn't do this out of religious duty, but because sin troubles her conscience and separates her from the Bridegroom's presence.[40] Separation from Him is miserable.

---

[40] 1 John 1:6-9

She goes to the throne of grace, not only to be able to cope with the challenges of life; she goes for grace to walk in holiness. This is in great contrast to the years when she walked in less love. She hates sin because it is not compatible with her desire for her Husband. The darkness of sin comes from the evil one, and she will not follow him. Her heart is sealed. She has eyes only for One. She is in love and will be satisfied only when she is found in His likeness.

Prayer:

Wonderful Father, You have seen me each time I have come to the throne of grace. The angels have looked and said, "Here she comes again!" And they have smiled. It has been a well-worn path for me these past months. You have held me and comforted me, but now, Abba, Father, I see what You have been creating in me with Your great love. I have been coming to You out of need and brokenness, but now a fire is rising in my heart. You have said, "Behold your Bridegroom," and You have placed my hand in His. You are my Father, giving me in marriage to Your Son, Jesus. Now there is a love that is more than I can describe, and I must have more. I know I have just begun to know the shallow shores of these deep waters that flow from Your throne. There are not words to describe what is happening in my heart, but I pray, "My Bridegroom! Take me to the deepest places of preparation as your bride. Help me clothe myself in fine linen, bright and clean by Your grace." I pray for grace not to shrink back or become distracted and complacent ever again.

FULLY KNOWN

"For your husband is your Maker, Whose name is the Lord of hosts; and your Redeemer is the Holy One of Israel, Who is called the God of all the earth" (Isaiah 54:5).

"For You formed my inward parts; You wove me in my mother's womb. My frame was not hidden from You, when I was made in secret, and skillfully wrought in the depths of the earth; Your eyes have seen my unformed substance; And in Your book were all written the days that were ordained for me, when as yet there was not one of them" (Psalm 139:13, 15, 16).

Marriage, at its best on earth, is only a shadow of a much greater and glorious reality in the eternal realm. While we are married to our earthbound mate, as wonderful as that union is designed to be, we are never able to be fully known in that relationship. There is always more to learn and sometimes forgive about each other. Jesus, the Bridegroom, the designer of marriage, knows all the needs of the human heart. His desire and plan are to fulfill those needs where man can only fall short. He says, "I'll be your Husband. I am the marriage. We will celebrate at the marriage supper of the Lamb!"

Embracing the Lord as our Husband is entrance into a more marvelous marriage than any marriage on earth. This is your Husband who fully knows you because He is your Maker! He knows you better than you know yourself, and He is delighted with you and your design. Having redeemed you with His blood, He sees you in the perfection of its cleansing power. You are His great beauty. He likes the way He put you together. You are delightful and precious. The secrets of your heart are laid bare before Him. When your heart's cry cannot find words, you can lean against Him and sigh, "Lord, You know. You know," and you are received in His love.

He is the Holy One, the God of all the earth, and you captured His heart before you came into existence. You have His eye. You are a masterpiece! He says you were skillfully wrought in the depths of the earth. In the depths of the earth? Yes! He saw you and designed you even before He formed Adam out of the dust of the ground. As if this was not enough, this wonderful Husband says that in His "books were all written the days that were ordained for me, when as yet there was not one of them" (Psalm 139:16).

Oh, this is a much better marriage than earth can endure! This is a marriage dwelling in the eternal realms of glory, bathed in the acceptance that every bride and groom longs for, where the future is already sealed in the unbreakable bonds of the blood of the Lamb. This is the true Husband. All else is a shadow.

Prayer:

Abba, Father, You have done it again! I am left feeling like a small child before You, with so much more to learn. You invite this child to accept the fact that she is a bride to her Creator. Thank You. Help me yield myself to the arms of Jesus in the revelation that I am known and treasured. Help me respond by seeking to know You. What a safe place of love You have created for me! Take me to the depths of this love. I want to explore Your heart all the rest of my days and then for all of eternity. Give me grace to seek You always. I love You, my Husband.

CLEANSED: RADIANT HOLY BRIDE

"Christ also loved the church and gave Himself up for her, so that He might sanctify her, having cleansed her by the washing of water with the word, that He might present to Himself the church in all her glory, having no spot or wrinkle or any such thing; but that she would be holy and blameless" (Ephesians 5:25b-27).

"Then He poured water into the basin, and began to wash the disciples' feet and to wipe them with the towel with which He was girded" (John 13:5).

We have been made righteous as though we never sinned by the blood of Jesus. But in Ephesians 5 the apostle Paul speaks of Jesus cleansing us "by the washing of water with the word." He says for this purpose Jesus gave Himself up; He died so He could sanctify us, setting us apart to holiness. Jesus demonstrated this cleansing by washing the disciples' feet on the night of His betrayal. It was an attentive, one-on-one ministry, as He took the posture of a servant at the feet of His bride. This is an amazing picture. Our Creator knelt as a servant before those He had created, to bathe their feet and make them presentable and acceptable to Him.

In Scripture, water symbolizes the Holy Spirit, so this "washing of water" with the Word involves the Holy Spirit being poured out on the Scriptures as we read them. Thus, the written word comes alive to us as we seek our Bridegroom, the Word of God made flesh.[41] As we read the Bible, our engagement with the Word becomes a living conversation that penetrates deep into the heart, so that it is alive within us, changing us.

This is much more than reading words on a page. This is an individualized one-on-one cleansing by Jesus while He speaks to our innermost being. This is different from listening to teachers or pastors. This is secluded and deeply personal. The Husband speaks to His bride in a place of intimate privacy with the purpose of presenting her to Himself without spot or wrinkle, flawless and holy. Oh, who would not want this tender care? Who would not want this glorious transformation, this beauty and holiness?

Prayer:

O Father, what a glorious gift of love You have provided in Your Son, Jesus. To think that I can know Him as

---

[41] John 1:14

my Husband, washing and cleansing and transforming me! Yes, Father, I pray for grace to come away for hours with my Bridegroom to be transformed as I read His Word. I pray for grace to press into this invitation of love. I want desperately to be this holy bride, not only by faith, but in full manifestation here on earth as I await His return. I want to be among those who radiate holiness as their beauty and adornment as I desire my Bridegroom! May I reflect His glory without spot or wrinkle. Yes, Lord, wash me with the washing of the water of the Word!

THE BRIDE AWAKENS TO HER BRIDEGROOM

"My soul waits for the Lord more than those that watch for the morning " (Psalm 130:6a, KJV).

"O satisfy us in the morning with Your lovingkindness, that we may sing for joy and be glad all our days" (Psalm 90:14).

"Cause me to hear thy lovingkindness in the morning; . . . .cause me to know the way wherein I should walk; for I lift up my soul unto thee" (Psalm 143:8, KJV).

When we have taken Jesus as our Bridegroom, our first thought when we wake up is, "Where are You, Lord?" Of course, He is there, and we know this by faith. He says He will never leave us or forsake us, but we want more. We want a tangible presence feeling His glory. We can't get out of bed and run hastily into the day because we must have Him first, and we awaken with our soul "waiting for the Lord more than they that watch for the morning" (Psalm 130:6).

We rearrange our lives so we have hours set aside for this special embrace with Him. We go to bed earlier so we can get up earlier. When He has become our Bridegroom, there is a passion that must be satisfied as we yearn for a deep drink of

His love. We call out to Him, "Cause me to hear thy loving-kindness in the morning" (Psalm 143:8). We must hear His voice, not only for instruction, but because we are in love. We are hungry for more of Him, and we must have a love encounter. Our soul is lifted up to Him, longing for Him, and we are thirsting for Him as our first love, above all else in the world. We want to feel His heartbeat!

Prayer:

Abba, Father, I come boldly to Your throne of grace and ask for help to pursue and not relent! I cry out for grace, Father. Let my heart be ignited and on fire for Jesus, not just as Savior, but as my Bridegroom. O Lord, I have lived with myself long enough to know I can become distracted and drift; I don't want any more of it. You have been so patient with me. I want all that You offer with Jesus. I want to experience what You mean when You say You are my Husband. Take me to the secret place; show me this mystery.[42] Teach me the way of it. Help me, Lord, and satisfy me with Your weighty, tangible glory so my heart and lips overflow with love in the hidden chambers of the secret place.

THE CHAMBER OF THE BRIDEGROOM

"One thing I have desired of the Lord, that will I seek: That I may dwell in the house of the Lord all the days of my life, to behold the beauty of the Lord, and to inquire in His temple" (Psalm 27:4 NKJV).

"When thou sadist, Seek ye my face; my heart said unto thee, "thy face, Lord, will I seek" (Psalm 27:8, KJV).

---

[42] Ps. 91:1, KJV

"The king hath brought me into his chambers: we will be glad and rejoice in thee, we will remember Your love more than wine" (Song of Solomon 1:4b, KJV).

David wrote fervently, "One thing I have desired of the Lord, that will I seek: That I may dwell in the house of the Lord all the days of my life" (Psalm 27:4 NKJV). He *did not say*, "That I may dwell in the house of the Lord *when I die and go to Heaven.*" For David to dwell in the house of the Lord meant to stay in His presence in constant communion with Him.

The bride, who cannot get enough of her Bridegroom's love, finds this dwelling place with Him now, here on earth. She has given herself to Him, and she leaves all distractions behind. She wants to dwell in His house permanently, never to leave or look to another. Her heart is welling up with desire for Him and Him alone. He is the love of her life, and His passion for her is all encompassing. He died to have her, and she has finally come into the revelation of how completely cherished she is.

Because she has awakened to this great love, she seeks daily to behold her Bridegroom's beauty and to inquire of Him. Yes, she has questions on her heart, but most of all His love is her sustenance, and she must be drinking this wine of Heaven. Oh, it is so much better than temporal wine! Any sense of separation is unbearable. This is the bride; she lives on the Bridegroom's love—conversation is an excuse to have His gaze.

In His chamber is where rejoicing finds fulfillment. He has been saying all along, "Seek My face," and she, at long last, has found what He has meant by this. For years it had been words on paper to her, but now she has broken through. No, she has not *just* found His presence; she has found the radiance of His love and joy streaming over her. How can she ever leave His arms?

She is no longer one knocking at His door with her needs and petitions. She is in the chamber of the King in His temple, and she is breathless beholding His beauty. Oh, she has come home! This is where she was created to be all along, and she has finally found her way by the leading of His hand.

Prayer:

Wonderful Father, I am left undone, not knowing how to respond to this promise of dwelling in Your house, except that my heart cries out, "Yes, Lord! Help me!" Pour Your grace upon me to enter this chamber of the Bridegroom. Help me press into this place each day until I know I have arrived in Your temple. Let it no longer be a distant faraway place, but let it be my permanent residence and condition of my heart to seek You face-to-face. Oh, bring me to the place of beholding Your beauty in Your temple as the bride. Yes, I do want to be this bride! I want to know the chamber of the Bridegroom and be seated with Him. By Your grace, may I hunger until I arrive at this habitation and drink this wine. Create in me a heart sealed in my Bridegroom's love, a heart that cannot pull away. I pray for grace, Abba, Father.

DELIGHTING IN THE BRIDEGROOM

"Like an apple tree among the trees of the forest, so is my beloved among the young men. In his shade I took great delight and sat down, and his fruit was sweet to my taste" (Song of Solomon 2:3).

"Delight yourself in the Lord; and He will give you the desires of your heart" (Psalm 37:4).

What bride is not delighted with her bridegroom? Song of Solomon says the bride took great delight and sat down in his shade, and his fruit was sweet to her taste. The passionate bride feeds directly from her beloved's hand, spending long hours with him, feeding on his word and she is delighted to do so. It is not a duty; it is her thirst.

This is wonderful imagery. It is the picture of a fresh love that has not grown old, where lingering with your lover is the "tree" of your choice. He is the tree of life, and his fruit is sweet. We must ask ourselves, "Do we *delight* in Jesus, or are we religious workers busily serving God?"

The stench of religion is what encased the Sadducees and Pharisees in Jesus' day. He was harsh in His rebuke of them, calling them a brood of vipers and their teachings leaven. Although they spent their lives poring over the Scriptures, they did not love God![43]

Jesus violently turned over the money changers' tables in the temple. To those who were selling the doves, He said, "Take these things away; stop making My Father's house a place of business" (John 2:16). Religion is a corruption that makes relationship with God a place of business where hearts have made Jesus their culture rather than their first love. I regret the years my heart was not centered on loving Him, and instead, I was content with "being a Christian." Oh, the stench of religion is a stench, indeed, before our God who paid such a price for us! He wants so much more for us. He wants to give us the desires of our hearts in this life as we align ourselves with delighting in Him. The desires of our hearts become pure in His shade, and He can respond to us because we flow in His will and travel with His heart. The carnal has lost its appeal to us. His purposes become ours.

In His great love He looks at us through the lens of the purifying blood of Jesus and says, "Delightful!" In His wonderful foreknowledge He sees us at the end of our journey, washed in the blood. We stand white as snow and pristine

---

[43] Matt. 12:34; 16:11

before Him, arrayed in purity and truth, free at last from the vestige of sin. While we are on earth, what a tragedy it is to miss Jesus as our passionate love, to miss the invitation to delight in Him as He delights in us.

Prayer:

Abba, Father, I pray for grace. Infuse me with Your spirit of joy for the Bridegroom, that I may respond to Your love, declaring from my heart, "In You is all my delight!" May I know as I awake each morning that I truly delight in You with a fresh and vibrant love. May I be ready to eat from Your tree and be held in Your shade. O Jesus, drench me in the fragrance of Your love. I love You.

CHAPTER 6

LITTLE FOXES SPOIL THE VINEYARD

CATCH THE FOXES FOR US

"My beloved responded and said to me, 'Arise, my darling, my beautiful one, and come along. . . (The fig tree puts forth and ripens her green figs, and the vines are in blossom and give forth their fragrance. Arise, my love, my fair one, and come away. [So I went with him, and when we were climbing the rocky steps up the hillside, my beloved shepherd said to *me*:] O my dove, while you are here in the seclusion of the clefts in the solid rock, in the sheltered and secret place of the cliff, let me see your face, let me hear your voice; for your voice is sweet, and your face is lovely.') Catch the foxes for us, the little foxes that are ruining the vineyards,

while our vineyards are in blossom"[44] **(Song of Solomon 2:10, 13-15).**

*S*ong of Solomon is a beautiful love song between the bride and the Bridegroom. But it carries a strong warning about how we must protect our relationship with Jesus if we are to stay close to Him. In this chapter we will focus on heeding this warning.

In Song of Solomon chapter 2, the vineyard (the relationship) is in full bloom, filled with beauty and fragrance. The bride has come away on a narrow path with the Bridegroom, and she is climbing—ascending higher—in her trust and love for Him. She is growing in her reliance upon Jesus as her Rock and safe place. She is hidden and sheltered in the secret place with Him, and He tells her how lovely she is to Him:

"|So I went with him, and when we were climbing the rocky steps up the hillside, my beloved shepherd said to me:| O my dove, |while you are here| in the seclusion of the clefts in the solid rock, in the sheltered and secret place of the cliff, let me see your face, let me hear your voice; for your voice is sweet, and your face is lovely" (Song of Sol. 2:14, AMPC).

The Bridegroom is enthralled with His bride! She has finally come close to Him. They are heart-to-heart, face-to-face in a secret place, and He doesn't want her to slip away from Him. As He looks deeply into her eyes, He tenderly warns her, in verse 15, to "Catch the foxes for us, the little foxes that are ruining the vineyards, while our vineyards are in blossom".

Who are these little foxes? They come at first as small thoughts, worries, fears and emotions designed to distract the bride and move her away from the narrow path she is on with Jesus. They are sent by the adversary to pull her away to a place where she has lost sight of her Bridegroom and the

---

[44] ( ) taken from AMPC

safety of His arms! If they can separate her from Him, they can rob her of peace and joy and prevent the vineyard from becoming fruitful.

It is the bride who must catch the foxes, or they will multiply and become destructive. She cannot mature in her relationship with God if she allows them to run unchecked in her life. The Bridegroom permits the invasion because, through testing, the bride grows in wisdom and strength. As the foxes come, she sees they tarnish her beauty and move her away from Jesus, so she becomes more diligent in her pursuit of Him, staying in close union with Him. The adversary is greatly threatened by this marriage spanning Heaven and earth. His demise is certain, as Heaven comes down in response to the hunger of the bride for her Bridegroom; so he continues sending his foxes—relentlessly—but the bride only becomes more skilled in taking them captive. With each victory she grows stronger!

Prayer:

Father, I come to You once again for grace. Help me not be intimidated by the fact that we have an enemy who wants to put a wedge between us. I am in a wonderful partnership with You—Father, Son and Holy Spirit, You are the all-powerful One, and I am in You and You in me. I trust You to teach me how to catch the foxes.

THE ADVERSARY

"Keep Satan from getting the advantage over us; for we are not ignorant of his wiles and intentions" (2 Corinthians 2:11, AMPC).

"Put on the full armor of God, so that you will be able to stand firm against the schemes of the devil" (Ephesians 6:11).

"We are destroying speculations and every lofty thing raised up against the knowledge of God, and we are taking every thought captive to the obedience of Christ" (2 Corinthians 10:5).

Jesus warns us about the devil, making it clear that we must learn how to defeat him. We don't mention him to glorify him, but we need to know the schemes of our adversary if we are to prevail over him. Paul gives us a stern warning in 2 Corinthians 2:11. He says don't be ignorant of satan's "wiles" lest he gets an advantage over us. In Ephesians 6:11 he writes, "Put on the full armor of God, so that you will be able to stand firm against the schemes of the devil." Then, in 2 Corinthians 10:5, Paul tells us that catching our thoughts is a vital weapon of our warfare against this enemy. He says, "We are destroying speculations and every lofty thing raised up against the knowledge of God, and we are taking every thought captive to the obedience of Christ." So there are schemes, wiles, devices, speculations and lofty things that rise up against the knowledge of God.

We don't want to be naïve and fail to catch them quickly. It is so much easier to defeat these invaders while they are small by taking their thoughts into captivity as soon as we are aware of them. If we allow the wrong thoughts to linger, they will grow into emotions and actions that undermine us.

By following this analogy of satan invading our vineyard with a pack of sly foxes, let's go to the throne of grace in prayer. Let's ask for the help we need to catch the foxes!

Prayer:

Jesus, I acknowledge that apart from You I can do nothing. I am surrendered to You as my help and my salvation, and I come to You, longing to abide in You as my Husband and Lord. I am so glad this includes You loving me passionately and calling me Your beautiful bride. Help me learn, as Your bride, how to catch the foxes when they come to spoil and ruin. Give me the grace to catch them while they are small. Help me get the revelation of how they work. I come to Your throne of grace asking for help. I don't want to be naïve and taken advantage of. I want to stay arm-in-arm with You.

THE FOX CATCHER

"He who dwells in the secret place of the Most High shall abide under the shadow of the Almighty. He shall cover you with His feathers, and under His wings you shall take refuge" (Psalm 91:1, 4, NKJV).

"But as for me, I shall sing of (Your mighty strength and power);[45] yes, I shall joyfully sing of Your lovingkindness in the morning, for You have been my stronghold and a refuge in the day of my distress" (Psalm 59:16).

As fox catchers, we are in a daily conflict. While I was praying one morning the Lord said that one strategy in war is to interrupt the communication system of the enemy. Then He pointed out to me how the devil was employing this tactic of war against me in the morning as I woke up. He was there with each dawn trying to scramble my communication with my Bridegroom. He might send memories directing my attention to the past, trying to cause me to grieve over what was gone, or He might try concerns about the future, trying to get my focus on what lies ahead. It may be as obvious as depression and worries, or fears and anxiety attacking me. The adversary's goal is to direct our focus away from looking to God and walking with Him, one day at a time. He continues this strategy of sabotage throughout the day.

The Lord said to me,

"The first priority in the morning is to come up here with Me. Push past all else and worship and praise and get in My glory. Come up here and nestle under My wing in the secret place. Don't be satisfied until you press through into the peace of My presence. Hear from Me first. Incline your ear to Me as I assure you of My love and pleasure in you. It is here you must abide all through the day walking with Me in My peace, and I will give you instructions as we walk together. The morning is a time to be satisfied with My lovingkindness."

As I pushed past the enemy's static of whispers and emotions into the arms of my Redeemer's love, these wonderful Scripture verses rolled through my mind:

"He who dwells in the secret place of the Most High shall abide under the shadow of the Almighty. He shall cover you with His feathers, and under His wings you shall take refuge" (Psalm 91:1, 4, NKJV).

"But as for me, I shall sing of (Your mighty strength and power);[46] yes, I shall joyfully sing of Your lovingkindness in the morning, for You have been my stronghold and a refuge in the day of my distress" (Psalm 59:16).

This is who we are as fox catchers. We start the day with Jesus, abiding under His wings, covered by His feathers and bathed in His lovingkindness. At night we declare His faithfulness because He has walked us through another day. The greatest victory of each day is to stay in His presence, abiding in His shadow in the secret place. In this position we are ready to catch foxes. In this place of light and glory they are easily exposed.

In the next chapter we will uncover some of the foxes. I suggest you read about them slowly—one or two at a time. Be patient. It takes practice and repetition to get our thoughts and emotions under control. With time we become resistant to the thoughts and emotional patterns of the foxes, and we prevail.[45]

Prayer:

O Father, how I love You! Help me. Give me grace to keep my gaze fixed on You and my ear attentive to Your voice. Help me be the bride who can think of none other than her Bridegroom. Help me get good at this. Help me quickly catch an intruding thought that takes me away from the peace of Your presence. Father, help me abide in the shadow of Your wings.

---

[45] I suggest you read *The Battlefield of the Mind* by Joyce Meyer.

CHAPTER 7

LET THE FOXHUNT BEGIN!

SORROW AND MOURNING FLEE AWAY

"A time to weep and a time to laugh; a time to mourn and a time to dance." (Ecclesiastes 3:4).

"You have turned for me my mourning into dancing; You have loosed my sackcloth and girded me with gladness" (Psalm 30:11a).

"Therefore the redeemed of the Lord shall return, and come with singing unto Zion; and everlasting joy shall be upon their head: they shall obtain gladness and joy; and sorrow and mourning shall flee away" (Isaiah 51:11, KJV).

When our loved one has gone to Heaven, sorrow and mourning are among the first enemies we contend with. Of course, there is "a time to mourn" (Eccles. 3:4).

Mourning speaks to the fact that we are in a fallen world where death exists because sin entered the world. We need to release our emotions with a flood of tears, but this time must come to an end. Bringing the time of mourning to an end speaks of the wonder of our salvation. We have great hope. We will see our loved one again. When I read that Joseph mourned Jacob for seven days and the Israelites mourned Moses for thirty days,[46] I decided to put mourning away after three weeks. I was still fragile and the trauma of being torn in half was real and long lasting, but for me, it was time to close the door to mourning. Sorrow and mourning can be stubborn. They masquerade as guests saying we must entertain them because we are widowed. They expect us to let them in. They say, "We belong here," but we can catch them before they take us into misery.

The Scripture says that sorrow and mourning flee away when we come with singing unto Zion (the heavenly Jerusalem), and we can obtain gladness and everlasting joy (Isa. 51:11). So, when sorrow would hit me with the sudden thought, "My husband is really gone," and mourning tried to come back through the door, I learned I didn't have to let them in. I decisively turned and sang praises to God instead.

I embraced Psalm 30:11, and I danced. "You have turned for me my mourning into dancing; You have loosed my sackcloth and girded me with gladness." I chose to "look not at the things which are seen, but at the things which are not seen; for the things which are seen are temporal, but the things which are not seen are eternal" (2 Cor. 4:18).

I looked at the fact that Nicky is alive as never before. I focused on the truth, that Jesus and Nicky are alive together, and I am alive in Christ as well. My husband's time on earth may have ended, but time is a vapor. Eternity is forever, and I am an eternal being in Christ as much as Nicky is.

---

[46] Deut. 34:8

Often at this time I said, "Father, I'm glad Nicky is so happy. Tell him I love him! Let all Heaven hear me shout that I love him." By declaring my ongoing love for him, I am coming to Zion and taking part in eternity. I believe my voice is actually heard in Heaven as I call to my Father. I believe it is very possible that my Abba-Father says to the angel messengers that serve Him,

> "Go tell Nicky Osborne that Margie is sending
> him her love again."

Maybe Nicky is looking in on me at the time, as a member of the cloud of witnesses. This is all speculation, but it is speculation rooted in the realities of Heaven. My imagination is aligned with imagining things in Heaven. It helps me stay rooted in the fact that as a Christian I am not of the kingdom of this world. I am of the kingdom of God. I will see Nicky again! We will walk on the streets of gold together!

Am I trying to talk with Nick? Am I praying to him? No, that is necromancy.[47] Demons have the ability to appear and impersonate people so we don't want to add this deception to our problems. There are cases where the Lord in His sovereignty has caught people up in a vision, and they have seen their loved one, but that is different.[48]

When I ask the Father to tell Nicky I love him, I am imagining the absolute reality of Heaven. I am placing myself there instead of receiving sorrow and mourning here on earth.

The scripture tells us that marriage does not exist in Heaven. Our marriage ended the day my husband died; but we will see each other in Heaven, and our capacity for love will far outshine anything we knew here on earth. Nicky and I will be at the marriage supper of the Lamb together, but I

---

[47] Deut.18:10-12
[48] Rev. 4:1, 2 Cor. 12:2

am no longer married to him. I have the best Husband: the eternal Husband. In the face of this greater truth, sorrow and mourning have been run out of my garden. Nicky is wonderfully alive in Christ, and I am alive in Christ. We are both the bride to the eternal Bridegroom, Jesus. We are in Christ for eternity. This is wonderful!

Prayer:

O Jesus, my wonderful Bridegroom, help me not fall back from this eternal reality! Help me, by Your grace, keep my mind in the heavenly kingdom and the facts of the truth of Your Word that my loved one is wonderfully alive. I am not left alone and helpless without him, but I am wonderfully married to You. When emotions rise up, this takes great grace, Jesus. Help me walk in the truth that I am of the kingdom of Heaven and not of this world. Help me stay up with You, far above sorrow. Help me live in the reality that my loved one has come to Zion, the heavenly city of God, and I have come to Zion also by faith. Sorrow and mourning are not for me! Help me, Father! Help me really grasp it and rejoice. Help me kick sorrow and mourning out of my day. Help me kick them hard and look to Heaven. This takes grace, Abba. Thank You for grace.

THE SPIRIT OF HEAVINESS

"Why art thou cast down, O my soul? And why art thou disquieted within me?" (Psalm 42:11 KJV).

"The Spirit of the Lord God is upon me; because the Lord hath anointed me to preach good tidings. . . . To appoint unto them that mourn in Zion. . . the garment of praise for the spirit of heaviness. . . ."(Isaiah 61:1a, 3 KJV).

"Giving them a garland instead of ashes, the oil of gladness instead of mourning, the mantle of praise instead of a spirit of fainting" (Isaiah 61:3a).

In Psalm 42:11, the psalmist asks the question, "Why am I cast down or disquieted?" He is alert even to be asking the question. At times I have dragged through the day apart from the joy and peace of the Lord without realizing I have drifted off course. When we *feel down,* it is a fox on the loose! He is sniffing around us to see if we will take his offer to forget who we are in Christ and accept the spirit of heaviness he is sending upon us. Isaiah 61:3 clearly defines heaviness or depression as a *spirit.* Isaiah is not using a figure of speech; he is exposing the enemy. Depression and heaviness are temptations; they are devils—foxes—knocking on the door of our thoughts and emotions.

They come along with other foxes, trying to build a nesting place in us, lined with unbelief and a measure of self-pity and discouragement, all of which are contrary to the goodness of God. They all carry misery with them. With the dawning of each day the Lord calls us to walk with Him, but depression is an intruder knocking on the door trying to get us to walk with him instead. Psalm 61:3 tells us it has been appointed to us to wear a garment of praise for the spirit of heaviness. It is an appointment from the throne of God. Each day is another day *appointed* for praise.

We don't want to entertain the spirit of depression, even briefly, because he is going to make us miserable. The Word says not to give an opportunity or place to the devil.[49] When the spirit of heaviness comes, he is asking for a place in us. To stop him, we don't open the door. We push his thoughts out of our minds, saying, "Get behind me, devil!" and we choose to praise and look at Jesus instead. I learned to shout, "Grace!"

---

[49] See Eph. 4:27, KJV.

and jump out of bed when depression was biting at me in the morning, and I sang praises to Jesus in defiance of this devil, no matter how heavy he felt. It was not easy; it was hard. But by the grace of God I could do it.

Prayer:

Abba, Father, I rejoice in You that You have redeemed me from the hand of the enemy. I pray for the grace to repent of depression. I pray for grace to be alert to satan's spirit of heaviness and grace to take up my appointed garments of praise instead. I accept my appointment. What a glorious assignment! How wonderful to be found as one praising You and releasing joy on the earth. Glory and goodness are Yours, Father. You have good plans for me, and I cast my cares on You. This takes grace, Father. I know I can't do it by myself. Without You it's impossible. Help me! Spirit of heaviness, "I say, Go!"

DISCOURAGEMENT

"Wait on the Lord be of good courage, and he shall strengthen thine heart: wait, I say, on the Lord" (Psalm 27:14, KJV).

"Be of good courage, and he shall strengthen your heart, all ye that hope in the Lord" (Psalm 31:24, KJV).

"Take courage, son; your sins are forgiven" (Matthew 9:2b).

"Daughter, take courage; your faith has made you well" (Matthew 9:22b).

You would be amazed at how many verses in the Bible say, "Take courage" or "Be of good courage."

Notice it says to *take* courage. Despite the thoughts that rage at us and the emotions that try to push us under, we have a choice to make. We can choose to push the emotions and thoughts aside and say, "No! I am not leaving the arms of my Beloved. I am holding onto His goodness and love over me. I refuse to be discouraged."

Even when feeling horrible, stupid and inept, we can rise up and say, "Praise God! Jesus, I trust You are with me. You are going to get me through as I lean on You. I take hold of courage. I choose it."

Jesus knows all about taking courage. With each step toward Golgotha He took hold of courage to continue His journey to the cross and our ultimate deliverance from satan. It took courage to lay His life down for ours. When He says, "Take courage," it is in us to do so (the ability is within us) because *He is in us.*

Jesus certainly had to refuse to obey feelings, thoughts and emotions on the way to the cross. As we cling to Him, refusing the fox of discouragement, Psalms 27:14 and 31:24 say He will strengthen our hearts. When Psalm 27:14 says, "Wait on the Lord; be of good courage," the Hebrew word for "wait" is from a root word in Hebrew meaning "to bind together." Now that is beautiful. We bind together with our Bridegroom, Jesus. We choose courage, and He strengthens our hearts.

Oh, this is good news, for we do not want to leave His side for a moment. As a widow, discouragement is a real enemy. Oh, it is so much better to be the bride of Christ, clinging to our Husband who will strengthen us!

Prayer:

Lord Jesus, I come running again to the throne of grace for help. Help me, Lord, to recognize discouragement when it tries to creep in. Help me catch it before it multiplies one thought after the other. Help me choose by Your grace to jump up and praise You instead and dance with my Beloved. Help me bind myself to You, cling to You, refusing to let go. Help me take courage. Help me choose to grab hold of it. Thank You that You hear me. Thank You that You will always help me when I call on You. I love You.

GRACE CAUGHT A FOX

"[Not in your own strength] for it is God Who is all the while effectually at work in you—energizing and creating in you the power and desire—both to will and to work for His good pleasure and satisfaction and delight" (Philippians 2:13, AMPC).

"The God of all grace, who called you to His eternal glory in Christ, will Himself perfect, confirm, strengthen and establish you" (1 Peter 5:10).

It is our Father who is at work in us, perfecting and strengthening us. When we see His handiwork in us begin to take shape in answers to our prayers it is very encouraging. One day, coming across Nicky's favorite pen in a drawer triggered an attack of grief. With the unexpected ambush the lump was in my throat again, and I was being offered a very bad rest of the day. Grief invited me to cave into uncontrollable sobbing, but instead of receiving the misery being offered to me I stopped short of its invitation.

Not by any power of my own, but by grace coming down from the Father, I was quick to obey when I heard God say,

"Don't go there; it's going to be miserable.
Remember to set your mind on things above."

I was surprised that I caught this fox so quickly. My surprise turned into praise and sparked the wonder of the goodness of our God. I had prayed just a few days before, "Father, help me not be caught by a surprise attack." I hated the way grief could come without warning. I was encouraged that God's grace was helping me, and resisting grief was becoming a quick reflex.

The attack was reduced to a brief interruption, and my thoughts returned to flowing with the Spirit of God. They were not run aground on the banks of the kingdom of darkness as I looked up and said, "Precious to the Lord is the death of His saints! My Nick is in absolute ecstasy! I am a citizen of Heaven, so I rejoice with Heaven. I am not of this world. Jesus, thank You that Nick is with You. I am happy He is whole and full of life and joy. I will see his face and look into his wonderful eyes again soon. I worship You, my God! Help me stay fixed in the reality of Your kingdom."

I thought of God's faithfulness and all the prayers I have prayed. He has heard them all. The answers to those prayers are being orchestrated in Heaven and will arrive here on earth in perfect timing. Isn't God's grace wonderful? Keep praying, and keep going to the throne of grace!

Prayer:

Thank You, Father, for grace. You are walking me through this, and the fox that came today is one fox that did not ruin our vineyard. Our vineyard is in bloom, and I am taking on the fragrance of Christ, my beloved One. Thank You, Father. It is true that with each temptation You make the way of escape for us.

JEALOUSY AND ENVY

"For where jealousy and selfish ambition exist, there is disorder and every evil thing" (James 3:16).

"The lines have fallen to me in pleasant places; indeed, my heritage is beautiful to me" (Psalm 16:6).

Eight of us sat around the table, enjoying a wonderful meal. Each of us was praying for breakthroughs in our lives, and we all were excited that the answers to our prayers were on their way.

Eighteen months later, I sat in the same restaurant with the same group of people at the same annual convention and watched as two of my friends celebrated their success in getting their programs on television, and a third was meeting with great success as well. I was now a widow, and my heart still ached for my husband. The awful sense that half of me was missing seemed as if it was never going to go away, and I was still having to fight ambushes of grief. I was continuously struggling to hold onto joy. Some breakthrough for me!

I wrote a quick note of congratulations to each of my friends later, but what was trying to gain root in me was unmistakable. Jealousy and Envy were making their approach to my heart. Following close behind, lurking in the shadows, was Self-pity. These were foxes that threatened to become as large as lions, and their appetites sought to devour my future and my joy.

"Catch the foxes for us, the little foxes that are ruining the vineyards, while our vineyards are in blossom" (Song of Sol. 2:15).

"Be of sober spirit; be on the alert. Your adversary, the devil, prowls about like a roaring lion, seeking someone to devour" (1 Pet. 5:8).

The Holy Spirit brought these verses to my mind and reminded me of my many prayers to stay alert and catch the foxes. He reminded me of my enemy who wanted to devour me. He reminded me of the danger of jealousy and selfish ambition that lead to disorder and "every evil thing." His warning to guard my heart rang loud and clear this time. I had come too far to take a wrong turn and bear the consequences that were sure to follow. It was hard enough to catch the little foxes. I didn't need "every evil thing" to come in the door too! Heavens, no!

Have you ever considered what a strong warning is given to us in James 3:16? "For where jealousy and selfish ambition exist, there is disorder and every evil thing." Every evil thing! I responded immediately, "Lord Jesus, I catch this fox and repent. Wash me clean by Your blood and help me never give into this wicked fox. I know You have good plans for me as Your bride. I choose to believe the future is good and bright with You. You have reserved pleasant places for me, and I want to walk there with You."

Prayer:

Abba, Father, thank You for giving me the grace to hear the voice of the Holy Spirit on this one. Thank You for the discerning of spirits. Instead of jealousy and envy, I say, Father, "the lines have fallen to me in pleasant places; indeed, my heritage is beautiful to me" (Psalm 16:6). Father, it is true Your eye is on the widow, and your ear is open to her cry. Thank You for Your wonderful plans for me. I know they are good. I am going to trust You for a good future.

DOUBT

"Beloved, if our heart does not condemn us, we have confidence before God" (1 John 3:21).

"Let us draw near with a sincere heart in full assurance of faith, having our hearts sprinkled clean from an evil conscience and our bodies washed with pure water" (Hebrews 10:22).

"If we confess our sins, He is faithful and righteous to forgive us our sins and to cleanse us from all unrighteousness" (1 John 1:9).

At times it just doesn't seem "to be working" when we sit down to worship, read our Bible and have our time with Jesus. We have known wonderful times with Him before, but now His presence isn't coming in a tangible way. We can't feel Him. Something is off-key. We have sought to start our day worshipping and aligning ourselves with God, only to sense that something is not right. We feel separated from Him, and then the thought creeps in that there must be something wrong with us. Then we feel less loved by God. Soon we feel discouraged.

"I am trying to be with You, Lord! Where are You? What is it about me that other people have so much more of You than I do?" We remember when we have failed in the past. Now we are in a full landslide, tumbling downhill. If we don't put the brakes on, we will plummet all the way to the bottom. At this point, foxes are frolicking all over the place, leaving their paw prints all over our white robes of righteousness, and we have fallen prey to some schemes and wiles of the enemy. The fox of Doubt came in when we couldn't feel the Lord, and then Self Depreciation leapt over the wall, followed by Jealousy wriggling through the hedge, and then here came Condemnation...again.

Jesus calls softly to us saying,

> "Remember, My Beloved, if your heart does not condemn you, you can have confidence when You come before Me. Check your heart" (see 1 John 3:21).

Okay, so it is time to take a look at ourselves. Is my conscience clear? Have I sinned so that I have moved away from God? Well, this is easy! What a relief, because if there is sin, the Word of God comes to our rescue again with, "If we confess our sins, He is faithful and righteous to forgive us our sins and to cleanse us from all unrighteousness" (1 John 1:9). This is wonderful! If we find any sin hidden in our hearts, we confess it, and we are "good to go."

More than likely we didn't find any sin, because we have been catching sins and confessing them as we walk step-by-step with Jesus. It was probably one of those times in which we were with Jesus and just as close to His heart as ever, but we had to enjoy Him by faith and not by our feelings. It is time to pick our confidence back up and draw near with a sincere heart in full assurance of faith, having our hearts sprinkled clean.

Our Father assures us that if we repent and confess our sins He is faithful to forgive us and cleanse us. Yes! We are confident of His love and our acceptance in His arms, whether we feel Him or not. We were being sabotaged by doubt.

Shaking off and refusing the voice of the accuser, with His doubts, is primary to our worship. The accuser is all about insulting the goodness of God as he tries to perch on our shoulder with his whispers and innuendos. Psalm 103:12 tells us our great and good God is so merciful that when we confess our sins they are removed from us as far as the east is from the west. We must believe Him. We don't have to carry the guilt of those sins again; they are gone and forgiven.

The accuser implies, "God is not *that* good. You are still guilty. God hasn't forgiven and forgotten." Well, he's a liar; we have caught that fox and driven him from our vineyard.

Prayer:

Oh, Abba, Father, You are compassionate and full of lovingkindness! I praise and exalt You and thank You that by the blood of the Lamb I am daily summoned to come into Your presence. Yes, I come and stay. I love You. I want to walk and shine in holiness. Oh, how my heart loves Your Spirit. Fill me more and more. Transform me more and more. When the darkness becomes darker in these last days, cause me to shine, shine, shine all the more. I lay myself before You and say, "Do Your surgery, Great Physician! Open me up, expose and fix me, and I will praise You all the more." I want the light of Your truth to fill me. I pray for grace to praise and sing and lift my voice today, high above the voice of the evil one, even if I feel absolutely nothing!

THE PRINCE OF CONDEMNATION: WHO LET HIM IN?

"There is therefore now no condemnation to them which are in Christ Jesus, who walk not after the flesh, but after the Spirit. For the law of the Spirit of life in Christ Jesus hath made me free from the law of sin and death" (Romans 8:1-2 KJV).

"It is the Lord your God who goes with you; He will not fail you or forsake you" (Deuteronomy 31:6b AMPC).

All of us have days when we are caught off guard, and the foxes seem to become ravenous wolves that devour us. Depression, fear, anxiety, anger, hopelessness, despair and an avalanche of thoughts, perceptions and emotions can hit us all at once, unexpectedly, and we cave in. We do not rise up, taking every thought captive like overcomers. We fail the test.

One time, coming home from a long trip, I fell headlong into all of the above. I had been traveling for many hours and was physically exhausted. I had let my guard down, thinking I could relax and rest. Instead I was thrown into a confrontation with a friend, and it did not go well. Tempers flared, and hurtful words were spoken. I was terribly disappointed in myself— deflated by my failure.

When we stumble like this, close on the heels of the ambush is the second wave of attack I will call "The Prince of Condemnation." He comes strutting in with his favorite weapon, which is a large, high-powered magnifying glass. He reminds us of every weakness and failure in our lives. Pounding on our minds and our emotions in feigned authority, he shouts, "You're not going to make it. You are worthless and guilty. One day you will even deny Christ when the pressure is on!" The prince of condemnation exalts himself above the throne of God, declaring himself to be our judge, while he magnifies our failure in our eyes.

He magnifies the degree of our failure with the hope that he can keep us down long enough to work deep discouragement in us. He even reminds us of the scripture that says God will not allow us to be tested beyond what we are able, and he drives home the point that we could have passed this test without sin if we loved God.

As the dust settled from the skirmish, I went before the Lord at the throne of grace; I prayed for all the people involved and cried out for grace for all of us. I confessed my sin of fear, lack of trust and the hurtful words I had spoken. Struggling to regain my balance, I began to worship and seek the presence of the Lord. The atmosphere changed around me, and for a moment my spiritual eyes were opened to see angels in the room with me! They had blond hair with pageboy haircuts and were wearing white robes with golden sashes. They were smiling.

At this point, I imagine satan is wringing his hands and kicking all his demons squarely on their behinds. I imagine he is ranting, "Oh, no, now she's going to get up stronger than ever." He is mercilessly beating the prince of condemnation and condemning him for failing in his assignment. It must have been quite a sight in the spirit world as the angels of God laughed at the foxes assigned against me.

Did I fail my test? I fell short of 100 percent but repenting and praying are not steps of failure. We are overcomers and champions in the making if we are determined to get up and keep running the race set before us.[50] I could have passed my test in excellence, but a fox had been working on me throughout my travels. I had failed to detect him. His whispers had weighed heavy on my heart for days setting me up for the ambush. He was quick to open the door to all the other foxes in the attack. He was dangerous. He had to be exposed and caught.

His name is "Alone."

Even though I was surrounded by people, I had felt terribly alone because my husband was gone. "Alone" is a special assignment against the widow and tries to accompany her every thought. He is a liar. When I came home, he loomed large ahead of me as I remembered how my husband used to greet me at the airport with flowers when I returned from a journey.

Jesus tenderly reminded me,

> "I will never desert you or forsake you.[51] You are never alone. My Spirit is in you, and My Father sealed you, giving His Spirit in your heart as a pledge."[52] Remember Romans 8 says, "Who will separate us from the love of Christ? Will tribulation, or distress, or persecution, or famine, or nakedness, or peril, or sword? . . . Neither death, nor life, nor angels, nor principalities, nor things present, nor things to come, nor powers, nor height, nor depth, nor any other created thing, will be able to separate us from the love of God, which is in Christ Jesus our Lord" (Rom. 8:35,38,39).

---

[50] Heb. 12:1
[51] Heb. 13:5
[52] See 2 Cor. 1:22.

I am not alone. I am never alone, not for a moment. I am with Jesus.

Prayer:

Thank You, Father, for delivering me from condemnation today. Thank You that it does not belong to me, even when I fall flat on my face. Thank You that sometimes, when I am discouraged with a failed test, You will let me see the angels You send to help me. I want to see them. It is wonderful that You send angels to us as You sent angels to strengthen Jesus when satan tempted Him in the wilderness. I was in a deep wilderness today, and You lifted me up. Please open my eyes to see more of the unseen world and help me to hear more clearly. I love the language of Your Spirit. I want more of this. Thank You for assuring me that I will never be alone. I want to cling to this reality and never let it go. Help me by Your grace never to be unaware of Your constant presence. I love You, Jesus.

RESISTING ANXIETY

"Anxiety in the heart of man causes depression, but a good word makes it glad" (Proverbs 12:25 NKJV).

"Rejoice in the Lord always; again I will say, rejoice! Let your gentle spirit be known to all men. The Lord is near. *Be anxious for nothing*, but in everything by prayer and supplication with thanksgiving let your requests be made known to God. And the peace of God, which surpasses all comprehension, will guard your hearts and your minds in Christ Jesus" (Philippians 4:4-7, italics mine).

According to Proverbs 12:25, anxiety *causes* depression. The apostle Paul was not anxious and worried when he was in prison. He knew better than to open this door to depression and despair. Instead, he wrote a letter to the church in Philippi, exhorting them to be anxious for nothing. He told them to take their problems to God with rejoicing and thanksgiving, trusting He would take care of them. He said to thank God in advance for the answers that were sure to come. Instead of anxiety they would have the peace of God. Paul said, "Rejoice in the Lord always; again I will say, rejoice!" (Phil. 4:4). The cure for anxiety is rejoicing and trusting God.

Paul was writing from the darkness of prison, but he maintained his joy and peace. The greater the darkness, the greater our need to refuse to be anxious and rejoice in God instead. Rejoicing aligns us with Heaven. There, rejoicing and praise explode around the throne of God in an everlasting flame of glory, exalting His goodness. When we embrace the fact that God is good we can't help but rejoice.

The foxes have been at work again if rejoicing does not fill our day. They have been clouding the concept that God is good and nudging us with their influence on our minds and emotions—those pricks of anxiety are from them. "Being anxious" is a devil at the door: "Knock, knock, knock! Let me in." Does he ever quit? No. But neither do we! We are overcomers.

When faced with problems we must learn to keep our focus on God and how good He is. Our God is awesome. His heart is that of a father for His children, in the highest and purest definition of the word. He came up with the idea of being a father. He is not a father to the angels, but He is Father to us. When He tells us to be anxious for nothing, He is saying,

"Just tell me what you need. I will take care of you."

First John 5:14, 15 says, "This is the confidence which we have before Him, that, if we ask anything according to His will, He hears us. And if we know that He hears us in whatever we ask, we know that we have the requests which we have asked from Him." The key concepts here are "confidence" and "asking according to His will." We find His will by studying the Bible.

I have learned it is good to write out a list of what I need and give the list to the Lord. This serves to remind me that I have decided not to worry about what I need. As God provides for me I check the items off the list. When I fail to be full of rejoicing, somewhere in my heart I am questioning whether or not God will come through for me. I am doubting His goodness. With this in mind, let's throw our arms around the goodness of God and embrace Him as our Abba Father, thanking Him for the answers to prayer before we see them.

Prayer:

Abba, Father, I repent. I am sorry to question Your goodness in my heart. I didn't know I was doubting You when I failed to "rejoice always."

Father, I pray for the revelation of Your great goodness to take root deep in my heart. I believe; help me with my unbelief.[53] Of myself, I can do nothing. Give me grace this day, to walk in the rejoicing that announces to everyone around me that my God is good and I am totally confident in Him. O Father, this is glorious! I have asked, so I have the requests I have made of You. I will rejoice all day. I will do it by Your good supply of grace. I will not insult Your goodness. In the name of Jesus, thank You. Thank You. Grace is being poured out on me to be alert and vigilant, to trust Your goodness and rejoice! GRACE, GRACE—I SHOUT GRACE TO THE MOUNTAIN OF ANXIETY, in Jesus' name! "Anxiety, get out!" In Jesus' name. "Go!"

---

[53] Mark 9:24

CHAPTER 8

THE FORGIVING LOVE OF GOD

WE ARE GIVEN THE MANDATE TO FORGIVE

"When they came to the place called The Skull, there they crucified Him. . . . But Jesus was saying, 'Father, forgive them; for they do not know what they are doing.' And they cast lots, dividing up His garments among themselves" (Luke 23:33, 34).

"Jesus said to them again, 'Peace be with you; as the Father has sent Me, I also send you.' And when He had said this, He breathed on them and said to them, 'Receive the Holy Spirit. If you forgive the sins of any, their sins have been forgiven them; if you retain the sins of any, they have been retained'" (John 20:21-23).

*A*lthough we will continue exposing foxes, understanding God's love and forgiveness is such an important subject that it deserves a chapter of its own. The foxes play havoc with us if they can trip us up in this area. Forgiveness is the essence of God's love. Not to forgive is to walk in the opposite direction of the heart of God. To grasp the importance of forgiveness, let us first look at Jesus.

Jesus hung on the cross in agony, stripped naked and crowned with thorns. His flesh was torn from His body, and His beard had been ripped from His face. Laboring to breathe and bleeding profusely, He looked down upon the soldiers casting lots for His clothes, and He said, "Father, forgive them; for they do not know what they are doing."

What an incredible view of the heart of God we are witnessing in this scene! In the height of His suffering, the Son of God hung between Heaven and earth, praying for mercy instead of judgment. He was not thinking of His suffering, although it screamed at him, from the crown of thorns on his head to the nails in His feet. Instead, His heart went out to those who were mocking and putting him to death. This is the picture of ultimate selflessness, ultimate love. This is the love of God shining forth in holy forgiveness from the cross.

After Jesus had risen from the dead, He appeared to the disciples, and John 20:22,23 tells us, "He breathed on them and said, 'Receive the Holy Spirit.'" He did not condemn them and remind them that they had all abandoned Him. Instead, He breathed the Spirit of life on them. Then He said, "If you forgive the sins of any, their sins have been forgiven them; if you retain the sins of any, they have been retained."

This is amazing! The first principle they are given as they receive the breath of God is forgiveness, and they are warned if they don't forgive sins, then sins are retained. This is powerful. Forgiveness is their first mandate. It is a key principle in the kingdom of God under the law of the Spirit of life in Christ Jesus.[54]

They had been prepared for this encounter beforehand. In Matthew 6:14, Jesus had said, "For if you forgive others for their transgressions, your heavenly Father will also forgive you. But if you do not forgive others, then your Father will not forgive your transgressions." In Matthew 18:35, Jesus said they would be turned over to the tormentors "if they did not forgive their brother *from their heart*" (italics mine).

They could not just give lip service to forgiveness. Forgiving others has to come from the heart. *It has to come from the heart of God in us by His grace.* With His help we can draw on His love that is in us because He lives in us. We can push past our emotions and pain and the complaints of our soul, and we can forgive. Just as Jesus forgave from His heart, so must we. Just as He chose not to be ruled by His suffering, we can choose not to be ruled by the suffering of an offense. We can forgive.

In Luke 6:28 we are told we must go even further than forgiving. Jesus says, "Bless them that curse you, and pray for them which despitefully use you" (KJV). This is the nature of God. When we arrive at the desire to bless and to pray for those who have wounded us, then we know we have forgiven from the heart. Then we know we have been delivered from the poison of unforgiveness separating us from Jesus.

Critical to catching unforgiveness is knowing it operates like a memory magnet to events in the past. It runs thoughts and emotions past your soul, enticing you to take hold and retain the poison of someone's sin against you. Unforgiveness wants you to relive the past, keeping the offenses alive. True love and true forgiveness will not take up these temptations but will stand firm with Jesus that these sins are removed as far

---

[54] See Rom. 8:2.

as the east is from the west and have no place in our minds.[55] Our spirit will say no to thoughts and memories offered on this plate of bitterness, for how can unforgiveness be joined to the One who came to forgive? How can we allow ourselves to be separated from our Bridegroom with something so opposite to His nature? After we have tasted His love, how could we bear it? We must forgive!

Prayer:

O Jesus, I cannot stand to separate myself from You with bitterness and unforgiveness. But, Lord, you must help me, for I have many wounds. Many people have disappointed me since my husband died. They don't have a clue how much pain I have been fighting. They don't know how hard it is to lose the love of their life. I forgive them. I pray You will strengthen me by Your Spirit in my inner man. Help me know the difference between the soul responding to offenses and the Spirit of life in Christ Jesus forgiving others from the heart. Give me revelation and grace to turn down the memories and emotions that lead the way on the road of bitterness. It is one or the other, isn't it, Lord? I operate in the law of the Spirit of life in Christ Jesus, or I step under the law of sin and death.[56] O Jesus, help me walk in Your love. Live in my heart. I open the door wide to You. I hear You knocking. I cry out, "Help me refuse the spirit of unforgiveness!"

REMORSE, GUILT AND REGRET

"And He replied to him, You shall love the Lord your God with all your heart and with all your soul and with all your mind (intellect). This is the great (most important,

---

[55] Ps. 103:12; Isa. 38:17b
[56] Rom. 8:2.

principal) and first commandment. And the second is like it: You shall love your neighbor as [you do] yourself.' "(Matthew 22:37-39 AMPC)

The great and foremost commandment is to love God with all our heart, soul and mind. Having taken Jesus as our Bridegroom, we are learning how to enter into this commitment of love in progressive stages of our development in Him. This is good, but there is also the second commandment.

Matthew 22:39 tells us the second commandment is like the first one: "You shall love your neighbor as yourself." With this verse the Lord is forthright in stating that loving Him goes hand-in-hand with loving our neighbor. Let's look more closely at this second commandment. It says we are to love our neighbor as our self. We must love *ourselves* as well as love God and love our neighbor. Here is the question we must address: do we love ourselves, or are we disappointed in ourselves and full of regrets that are biting at our heels as we try to walk in love with Jesus? Are remorse, guilt and regret rising up from the past?

I was floundering under a bombardment of thoughts and emotions being thrown at me one day by these three tormenters. I was so sorry for the ways I thought I had failed my husband while he was alive. I regretted things I could have handled differently while he was sick. I thought of things I wished I had done. Then I thought of things I wished I hadn't done. Now it was too late. He was gone. My daughter helped me with this one day when she said, "Mom, Dad is so free in Heaven he doesn't even care what happened or what he suffered. Everything is forgiven in Heaven. He just loves you!" I remembered my experience with the fire of God's love after Nicky went to Heaven, and I knew my daughter was right.

But then the troubling thoughts rolled around to regretting some of the decisions my husband and I had made before he became ill. I was still living with the effects of some of these decisions. If we had known the future, we would have done things differently. I was wallowing in this mire of disappointment with myself and rapidly losing perspective when the Lord confronted me. He said,

> "Margie, you are not forgiving yourself. You are not loving yourself. Watch out! By not forgiving yourself, you are saying you don't embrace the price My Son paid for you. Instead of hearing My voice, you are listening to satan's voice when you carry these regrets. He is not only enticing you to doubt Me and My forgiveness, but he is tempting you to set yourself above Me and reject My ways. It is sin."

Now that surprised me. I had not looked at entertaining remorse, guilt and regret as entertaining sin. The Lord said,

> "Love yourself, forgive yourself, and leave it behind. Don't allow thoughts to take you in this direction. Don't regret these things of the past—and that would mean things from just yesterday or even an hour ago when you were disappointed in yourself. All this disappointment is not from Me. Keep going forward."

We must press forward. Oh, this is much better! All this regretting the past is torture.

Prayer:

Abba, Father, I am so grateful You are exposing the snares of the evil one. Father, I worship and magnify Your great goodness. You are glorious. You are Love! All praises belong to You, and I offer up to You my forgiveness of myself. I repent of entertaining remorse, guilt and regret, and I cast them aside into the place of "forgotten." Forgotten for eternity! In the name of Jesus, I am forgiven. Forgive me, Father, for this sin of setting myself above You...against the greatness of Your forgiving heart of love. Father, I pray for grace to stay reminded of this, and I pray for grace to forgive and love others from my heart. I pray for grace to genuinely desire to see them delivered and blessed. Thank You, Father. I go out today rejoicing! Thank You for this wonderful freedom. I am forgiven, and I forgive myself. In Jesus' beautiful, all-powerful name, I pray.

JUDGING OTHERS

"Then Moses returned to the Lord, and said, 'Alas, this people has committed a great sin, and they have made a god of gold for themselves. But now, if You will, forgive their sin—and if not, please blot me out from Your book which You have written!'" (Exodus 32:31, 32).

"I have great sorrow and unceasing grief in my heart. For I could wish that I myself were accursed, separated from Christ for the sake of my brethren. . .who are Israelites, to whom belongs the adoption as sons" (Romans 9:2-4a).

While Moses was on the mountain receiving the Ten Commandments, the Israelites quickly returned to idolatry. They made a golden calf and celebrated and sang and bowed down to it in worship, saying it was the god that had delivered them from Egypt. God was enraged and ready to destroy them all, but Moses intervened. He reasoned with God on their behalf and asked Him to forgive their sin. He even asked to be erased from God's book if He would not forgive the Israelites. He interceded for them as a type of Christ, saying,

"Forgive their sin—and if not, please blot me out from Your book which You have written!" (Exod. 32:32).

The apostle Paul was stoned and beaten; the Jews tried to kill him many times because he proclaimed Jesus was the Messiah. His response was to say, "I have great sorrow and unceasing grief in my heart. For I could wish that I myself were accursed, separated from Christ for the sake of my brethren" (Rom. 9:2-3).

Both Moses and Paul demonstrated the heart of Jesus. God would much rather have mercy than bring judgment. He is also the God of justice, and because justice demands judgment Jesus came and bore the judgment for us. Through Jesus, God devised a plan to satisfy justice and mercy at the same time for those who will repent and receive it. God is amazing!

While I was praying one morning, I was struggling with many things that were hard to forgive. Things I wished had not happened kept crowding my emotions. I was being careful to keep forgiving and praying for some people who had caused my husband and me great harm for many years and who continued to dishonor his memory even after he was gone. This ate at me. It was troubling and made it hard to leave the past behind. Then there were those who had hurt me while I was widowed and while my defenses were weakened by the trauma I was in.

I had been fasting and praying, and I was sure I had finally forgiven them; so Abba, Father began to deal with me. He dealt with me first about whether I cared if these people met with calamity. Did I want them to reap judgment for what they had sown, or did I want mercy for them? This was the hard part; what they had done was outrageous and vicious. Surely they needed to get a taste of the deep pain they had caused, so they could learn from it. The Lord was concerned about the hard place He saw in my heart, so He reasoned with me saying,

"If you want to talk about outrageous, Margie, wasn't it outrageous for the Israelites to run to an idol after their great deliverance from Egypt? Not only did they witness the plagues I sent upon Egypt and the great night of the Passover, but I opened the Red Sea for them. I healed all their sick so there was not a feeble person among them; yet look how quickly they turned away from Me. I was ready to destroy them, but Moses as a type of My Son stood between them and Me and said, 'Blot me out instead!'

"If you want to talk about vicious, how vicious was it for the Jews to drag Paul outside the city and stone him, leaving him for dead? They thought they had killed him; yet Paul wished he could be accursed if it would save them."

I wrestled with myself, and I saw what God was illuminating in my heart. I was not forgiving at all, unless I desired mercy instead of judgment for others. It was one thing to say I forgave them, but what did I desire for them in my heart? I was not forgiving unless I could say from my heart, "Father, do not judge them on my account. Father, it would break my heart to see calamity come upon them. It would hurt me to see them suffer. It would pain me to see them reap what they have sown." God wanted me to take the position of praying for them to be saved out of darkness and brought into the kingdom of God. Christianity is about forgiving. As believers, we always have to deal with forgiving people; it is ongoing and foundational to our faith.

Prayer:

Father, again I am amazed at Your great love and mercy for those You have created. I am seeing I have just begun to learn Your ways. Forgive me for the hardness of my heart, and help me, Lord. I am seeing seeds of corruption toward many I thought I had forgiven. I have prayed for You to bless them, but I have had a subtle satisfaction in seeing trouble come into the lives of some of the people who have troubled me. I have felt a sigh of disappointment when others prospered who had hurt me. I have fallen for another fox. He says, "Have mercy on me, but not so much mercy on others."

I see I will have to revisit the list of those I have forgiven and finish the job. I am made sober by Your correction, and I thank You for it. Lord, help me clean it all up. I pray for grace to forgive from my heart and thank You for it in the name of Jesus.

CHAPTER 9

STRENGTH AND VICTORY ARE IN THE VINE

TIME TO TAKE A BREAK

"I am the vine, you are the branches; he who abides in Me and I in him, he bears much fruit, for apart from Me you can do nothing" (John 15:5).

"If anyone does not abide in Me, he is cast out as a branch and is withered" (John 15:6a, NKJV).

"But the Lord is faithful, and He will strengthen and protect you from the evil one" (2 Thessalonians 3:3).

In our study we are in danger of falling flat on our faces under a load of dos and don'ts. It is time to take a break and make sure we are on the right foundation. Jesus said, "I am the vine, you are the branches; he who abides in Me and

110

I in him, he bears much fruit, for apart from Me you can do nothing" (John 15:5). I have mentioned this verse before. Going to the throne of grace for help is a constant exercise in leaning on Jesus to live through us. As we get stronger, however, I find that I need to be reminded again not to do things by my own strength. This is especially true for me now that I am past the initial challenges of being widowed.

When we revert to self-effort we are doomed to fail in things of the kingdom of God. We have stepped away from the living relationship of our being dependent on the life of Jesus Christ flowing through us like the branches that are attached to the vine. The branches that dry up and become "withered" (John 15:6a) do so because they have lost their attachment.

Self-effort is religion instead of relationship. A subtle shifting away from total dependence on Jesus in every part of our lives is a directional miscalculation that must be pulled into alignment. Just as a ship must stay on course if it is to reach its safe harbor, so must we. That is why Jesus uses the analogy of *walking* with Him throughout the Bible. For example, in John 12:35, Jesus said to them, "Walk while you have the Light, so that darkness will not overtake you." Step-by-step we must check our course. Are we connected to the Vine, and it is no longer "I who live but Christ who lives in me"?

The secret to overcoming religious efforts that derail us is to fully recognize what Jesus said so simply in John 15:5. He said, "Apart from Me you can do nothing." Often we reserve this verse for big things in life rather than for our every step. For example, we may read that "faith comes by hearing and hearing by the Word of God,"[57] so we go for it. We decide we are going to read the Bible daily and get the faith we need. In our own effort we may start out strong, but eventually we discover we are not arriving at the high goal set before us.

---

[57] Rom. 10:17 NKJV

Before we know it we haven't read the Bible in days. Our mistake is self-effort.

As we run back to the Vine and throw our dependence to accomplish anything that is fruitful on Him we find the truth of 2 Thessalonians 3:3: "But the Lord is faithful, and He will strengthen and protect you from the evil one". He doesn't strengthen us so we can walk without Him. He strengthens us to walk " in Him". He is the One doing the work of our lives conforming us to His image. He is the source that produces the fruit of victory in any challenge.

Prayer:

Lord Jesus, I come to You and ask for grace to come to the throne of grace. I ask for grace this day to walk step-by-step in awareness of drawing life from You. Grace to pray, to read, to get dressed and get to work, to make the right decisions. Grace to obey all the truth You have shown me so far. Help me be like a child holding on to You each toddler step of the way until I am so seasoned in my dependence on You that I run like a champion by Your side. May I run like a champion who is the reality of Christ living in me, the hope of glory. I love You, Jesus.

CHAPTER 10

PRAISE MAINTAINS THE PRESENCE OF THE BRIDEGROOM

THE ATMOSPHERE OF HEAVEN

"I will bless the Lord at all times; His praise shall continually be in my mouth. My soul shall make its boast in the Lord; the humble shall hear of it and be glad. O magnify the Lord with me, and let us exalt His name together" (Psalm 34:1-3 NKJV).

"Through Him, then, let us continually offer up a sacrifice of praise to God, that is, the fruit of lips that give thanks to His name" (Hebrews 13:15).

I have mentioned praise throughout my story. I want to bring it into sharp focus in this chapter. One way we maintain the presence of our Bridegroom and stay in step with Him is by establishing an atmosphere of praise around us. He inhabits our praises. He is enthroned upon our praises. Praise attracts Him and invites Him; so, regardless of our circumstances, it is always time to offer extravagant praise to the Lord. Psalm 34:1 describes the lifestyle of praise found in the Bible. "I will bless the Lord at all times; His praise shall continually be in my mouth." No matter what comes our way we bless the Lord and praise Him. We magnify Him and exalt His name above all else.

When my husband was diagnosed with stage four cancer, I lay on our office floor overwhelmed and crying out to Abba-Father that I didn't think we were equal to this one. We had been caught short on faith. I almost couldn't breathe as I agonized in prayer. To my surprise, the Lord responded immediately. He spoke clearly to me in a voice that penetrated my whole being. It was unmistakable. He said,

> "Margie, this is not too hard for you. You simply do what I have already taught you to do. You praise Me."

To this day, I am grateful He made His voice so clear to me. I went to war for my husband's life with praise and worship. Although Nicky and I faced many difficult things until he went home, we had the atmosphere of Heaven surrounding us in an amazing way. The Lord's presence was thick on us, and we did not suffer defeat in any sense of the word. We were in a terrible battle, but we were not defeated. I played praise music night and day and sang and worshipped God, no matter what, no matter where—everyone we encountered knew we were praising God. Praise was the best thing I did for my husband. It lifted both of us up.

Once, in the middle of the night, Nicky couldn't breathe, and we were rushed by ambulance to the hospital in Louisville. It was an hour-and-a-half drive going high speed with sirens blaring. Nicky needed so much oxygen that the medics were worried we couldn't get there before they ran out of the maximum supply they could carry. They put me in the front of the ambulance, and as the cold chills of fear tried to consume me, the Spirit within me said,

"Praise now!"

I turned to the ambulance driver and said, "The Lord just told me to praise Him, and that's what I am going to do." In a loud voice I praised, and I sang and declared Scripture so Nicky could hear me above the sirens. I declared the gospel and the kingdom of God all the way into the emergency room. It was an act of sheer will, but I did it by the grace of God. We praised through the night when he was in pain, and we praised through difficult medical procedures. When the doctors drew the fluid off his lungs with a long needle, we held hands and looked into each other's eyes, praising Jesus. The doctors were amazed when Nicky didn't flinch in pain. Later, one doctor said in awe, "You are a man of God, aren't you." It was a statement, not a question.

We praised God with each bad report. We praised through tears. We did not stop. When the battle for life on earth was exhausted, and I had to face losing the "love of my life" to Heaven's gates, the Lord said to me again,

"Margie, this is not too hard for you. You simply do what is already in you. You praise Me."

So, while Nicky is dancing in extravagant worship and joy before the throne of God in all of Heaven's glory, I dance and praise Him extravagantly here on earth. Is it a discipline? Is it hard? Yes, at times it is extremely hard for my flesh and emotions to obey my choice to praise, but the Spirit of God responds, and the glory of the Lord carries me in amazing grace. Do I fall away from praise at times? Yes, and the Lord says,

"Remember what I have been teaching you."

Do you want God to show up? Do you want to walk arm-in-arm with your Bridegroom above your problems? Praise Him! Let there be an irresistible invitation of praise ascending to Heaven's throne, inviting the Spirit of God to move in your life.

If we choose to praise when we don't feel like it, we enter into a whole new dimension. We join the company of those who are looking to the eternal city of God. Remember: "Here we do not have a lasting city, but we are seeking the city which is to come" (Heb. 13:14).

Prayer:

Father, I know I can't praise You on this level, except by Your grace. This is impossible without Jesus living through me. Help me do it. Help me live in a higher dimension with You.

PRAISE AND THE REJOICING OF HOPE

"Hold fast the confidence and the rejoicing of the hope firm unto the end" (Hebrews 3:6b, KJV).

"Behold, the eye of the LORD is on those who fear Him, On those who hope for His lovingkindness." (Psalm 33:18).

"Therefore I will offer sacrifices of joy in His tabernacle; I will sing, yes, I will sing praises to the LORD" (Psalm 27:6b, NKJV).

I am blessed with a great son-in-law. He is a wonderful father. My three little grandsons run to greet him when he arrives home because they trust him. In their eyes he can solve all problems and fill every need. Giggling and clamoring to get on his lap for hugs and play, they are a picture of God's children trusting Him in the kingdom of God. I've watched this scenario many times and heard the Lord say,

> "This is how I want you to come to Me, Margie. Come to Me like a child, rejoicing in hope, knowing I hear You and will supply all your needs."

This is much better than being tangled up in doubtful thoughts and emotions offering us a miserable day. We can have hope—a joyful confident expectation—that God's goodness will be there for us every time we go to Him. Joy and hope go hand-in-hand with praise and singing. Hebrews 3:6 tells us to hold fast to the rejoicing of hope. To me that means, "Hold on tight!" As we praise and rejoice in hope we draw the attention of our Father. Psalm 33:18 says, "The eye of the Lord is on those who fear Him, on those who hope for His lovingkindness." What better place could we be than under His watchful eye? Certainly, this is cause for celebration as we bring our sacrifices of joy and praise to Him. Psalm 27:6 says, "I will offer sacrifices of joy in His tabernacle; I will sing, yes, I will sing praises to the Lord" (NKJV).

Prayer:

O Father! Even though my emotions are still shredded at times, I repent of coming to You in doubt and worry instead of rejoicing and hope. I don't want to insult Your goodness and faithfulness by accepting fear about the future any more. Help me by Your grace to be infused with an attitude of hope looking to a future filled with Your good plans for me. Help me hold fast the confidence and rejoicing of hope firm unto the end. I love You, Jesus. Help me be radiant with joy. I can't do this without You. Help me, Lord!

ANGELS

"Truly, truly, I say to you, you will see the heavens opened and the angels of God ascending and descending on the Son of Man" (John 1:51).

"For he will give his angels [especial] charge over you to accompany and defend and preserve you in all your ways. . .They shall bear you up on their hands, lest you dash your foot upon a stone" (Psalm 91:11,12 AMPC).

"Are not the angels all ministering spirits (servants) sent out in the service [of God for the assistance] of those who are to inherit salvation?" (Hebrews 1:14 AMPC).

During the year I lived at the farm preparing it for sale the Lord sent His angels to guard and help me. One day I stood at the sink, crying. I had mixed my protein drink in my blender, and a vacuum had formed in the canister. I couldn't get the lid off. With all my might I couldn't budge it. In despairing loneliness I gave into frustration and tears.

Outwardly it seemed like a "small crisis," but it was amplified by the fact that my children had not called me for days. For them the grief of their father's passing was healing with time, and their lives were busy. For me, however, it was doubly fresh as I dealt with selling our farm and going through Nicky's things. What to keep—what to give away. It all made me cry.

The day before, I had almost fallen backward off the porch as I scrubbed mildew off the rails. The thought that I could have lain in the heat with an injury and no one would have missed me added to my isolation. So there I stood at the sink with a lid I couldn't unscrew, caving into the emotional cascade of the moment.

I had spent two hours worshipping and praying that morning, but no great sense of God's presence had come. The atmosphere in the house was better, but I didn't feel His glory. Why wasn't He responding to me? And now I couldn't even get the lid off!

"God, You said You are my Husband. Where are You? I need angels to unscrew this lid!" I wasn't angry. As I write this my words look angry on paper, but that wasn't the case. I was fragile and unstable with the nagging hollowness of still feeling like half of me was gone. Was it ever going to end? So much of what I used to be capable of just wasn't there anymore. I needed help and reassurance.

The year before, a widow had told me how angels had helped her on a regular basis. I was skeptical, but with tears I said, "You did it for her, Lord! Your angels helped her. Do it for me, too. Please help me get this lid off!"

I tried the lid one more time, and it easily unscrewed in my hands. "O Jesus, You did it! You did it!" Now my tears were tears of relief and joy. In that moment Jesus, my Husband, said to me,

> "Go write this down while it is fresh. I don't want you to forget it. My widows need to know My angels are there for them. They must keep the stairway into Heaven open over them with praise and worship so my angels can move freely ascending and descending from Heaven on their behalf. They have been here with you all the time. By the way, it was my angel that kept you from falling off the porch yesterday.

Have you forgotten how my angels saved you
when you were thrown from your horse?"[58]

From that day forward, anytime I needed help I asked God
to send His angels to help me. I ask for their help to this day.
They not only help with lids on jars and keep me from falling;
they have saved me from accidents while driving from Texas
to Maine to see my children and grandchildren more times
than I can count.

Prayer:

Jesus, You are so good! Thank You for sending the angels.
Help me keep busy about the business of praising and singing
to You. What a delightful way to walk with You!

---

[58] Ps. 91:12 (see Introduction).

CHAPTER 11

GRACE MULTIPLIED

MORE HELP THAN WE COULD IMAGINE

> "Grace to you and peace, from Him who is and who was and who is to come" (Revelation 1:4).

> "Grace and peace be multiplied to you in the knowledge of God and of Jesus our Lord" (2 Peter 1:2).

> "For of His fullness we have all received, and grace upon grace" (John 1:16).

Did you know we can have grace multiplied to us? We can have grace upon grace. Why do we even try to do things by our own strength when our Father has made so much help available to us? Why do we try to walk independently of God?

In three of the last years of my husband's life, Jesus extended grace to me by taking me through some serious "training" to prepare me for what was coming. When we moved from Texas to Kentucky, Nicky expected to get work nearby;

121

but when the jobs didn't come he had to travel for work. In our wonderful marriage we did everything together, so we were miserable when separated. To overcome this, the Lord told us to choose to rejoice and praise Him each time Nicky drove out of our driveway for a job away from home. We did this as an aggressive strategy because the alternative was terrible depression. I would stand on the porch waving and throwing kisses, and we would cheerfully say, "Good-bye."

Contrary to our plans, I was thrown into a difficult season of being alone for weeks at a time. Living nine miles away from our new town I was isolated and without friends. I cried out, "Grace, Father, give me grace! Help me choose to be happy and cheerful and rejoice instead of being miserable." Little did we know I was being trained to walk without Nicky.

After Nicky went to Heaven and I had to spend a year at our farm before it sold, I was grateful God had prepared me to be there by myself. I whispered, "Thank You," to Him many times, as I realized He had taken me through a dress rehearsal. I had been on this stage before and was trained to rejoice. It was much harder of course, but God increased His grace on me to bear it. I thought to myself, *Well, this is like when Nick was gone on a job. The Lord was getting me ready for this.* I was rehearsed in choosing a good attitude while waiting for my husband's return, and now I was waiting again. It was another season of waiting to see Nicky. This time, it was in the larger, eternal scheme of things: waiting for the day when I would see him in Heaven. God had trained me to wait with good expectation. He had multiplied grace to me!

After the farm sold and months stretched into years, I began to struggle with living alone. I was in a new town without friends and I had fallen into looking back instead of forward. I let go of joy, and grief was very willing to come through the door again. I couldn't pull out of it. I went to a wonderful woman of God for prayer and bluntly told her, "I am not making it. I don't have enough grace for this."

She said, "Margie, you are recycling in grief. You must stop looking back, receive God's great love for you and believe He has good plans for you. We are going to pray for a much greater measure of grace for you, and God is going to give it to you." I needed grace multiplied to me again, and He did it. A greater measure of grace came on me, and I was able to go forward again.

God is so good to prepare us by grace, to give us *more* grace and then to *multiply* grace. Grace is wonderful! As Peter said, "Grace and peace be multiplied to you." Think about that. Grace is multiplied to us. According to John, we can have grace upon grace. We can have God help us beyond what we can imagine in every situation.

Prayer:

Glorious Abba, Father, I come to You today and ask for more grace. I thank You for it. I celebrate Your grace. I say, "Yes, Lord, multiply grace and help to me!" I ask for grace to choose not to be miserable. Give me grace to be determined to finish out this day having followed Jesus. Thank You that You are mindful I am but dust. I am sure aware of it,[59] but You say I am transformed dust. I am a new creation in Christ, and You are helping me. Thank You that You have prepared me for this day. Open my eyes to see how, in fact, Your plan has been at work rehearsing me for this time in my life. You have set things in place so that life is not impossible for me. I can do it—with You. Thank You, wonderful good Father!

---

[59] Ps. 103:14

CHAPTER 12

A WONDERFUL GIFT

THE KINGDOM OF HEAVEN INVADES EARTH

"When the day of Pentecost had come. . .suddenly there came from heaven a noise like a violent rushing wind, and it filled the whole house where they were sitting. And there appeared to them tongues as of fire distributing themselves, and they rested on each one of them. And they were all filled with the Holy Spirit and began to speak with other *languages*, as the Spirit was giving them utterance" (Acts 2:1-4, italics mine).

"Now there were Jews living in Jerusalem, devout men from every nation under heaven. And when this sound occurred, the crowd came together, and was bewildered because each one of them was hearing them speak in his own language. . . . 'We hear them in our own tongues speaking of the mighty deeds of God'" (Acts 2:5, 6, 11).

*O*ur God knows how to invade earth with the kingdom of Heaven! Think about it. Isn't it amazing that Jesus came from the invisible realm of Heaven and brought the kingdom of God to earth? Meditate on that for a minute! Fallen man was trapped in a finite and physical world, confined to time and destined for death, but Jesus came bringing the eternal realm of the kingdom of God. While He was here, He performed numerous supernatural signs and wonders to represent the Father and prove He was not of this world. He healed every kind of disease, raised the dead, walked on water and turned water into wine to name a few. Every day He demonstrated the supernatural power of God. When He left earth, the Father sent the Holy Spirit[60] in His place to continue Heaven's supernatural invasion of the fallen world. In John 20:22 Jesus met with His disciples after His resurrection, and "He breathed on them and said, 'Receive the Holy Spirit.'" I believe this was when they were born again by the Spirit of God. But this wasn't enough. He had more for them.

Right before He ascended into Heaven, Jesus told the disciples to wait in Jerusalem until the Holy Spirit came *in power*. He told them they would speak in unknown languages and be empowered when this happened. He told them to be sure to wait for the Holy Spirit to come before they tried to preach the gospel.[61]

When the Holy Spirit came, He made a dramatic entrance with the sound of a violent rushing wind, and visible tongues of fire appeared and rested on each of the disciples. The scripture doesn't say there was a wind. It says there was the "sound" of a violent wind. Thousands came running to see what it was! They were astonished to hear those who had been waiting for the Holy Spirit, speaking in the 16 different languages of the foreigners who had come to Jerusalem for Pentecost.[62] And

---

[60] John 14:26
[61] Acts 1:4-9
[62] Acts 2:9-11

what was being said? The mighty deeds of God were being exalted! The Holy Spirit, speaking supernaturally through the disciples, spoke of the mighty deeds of God! From that day forward the disciples were empowered to preach the gospel without fear, even when threatened with death. Much is to be said about the empowerment and gifts of the Holy Spirit, but of particular amazement to me is the gift of speaking in tongues.

The Holy Spirit comes inside us and speaks through us in a language we don't know, bypassing our natural mind. Now that is a lot of proof that something out of this world has happened! It is that simple and it is a big part of the supernatural invasion of Heaven on earth. Amazing. Why speak in a language we don't know?

First of all, we need help with our prayers. Paul addresses this weakness in Romans 8:26, 27: "In the same way, the Spirit also helps our weakness; for we do not know how to pray as we should, but the Spirit Himself intercedes for us with groanings too deep for words. . .because He intercedes for the saints according to the will of God."

This is incredible! God Himself will pray through us and for us when we don't know how to pray. Have you ever come to God with needs so deep you didn't know how to articulate them? That was certainly my condition, as I dealt with the aftermath of my husband leaving for Heaven. My needs were too much for me to put into words. My whole world had changed, and there were groanings in the deepest part of me. What a relief that my loving Father anticipated my need and provided me with the gift of a supernatural prayer language. I could pour my heart out before Him in perfect prayer.

I was desperate to emerge victorious and pleasing before Him in the most difficult trial of my life, and He was there to help me pray. Amazing. He has thought of everything, even praying for us, through us. Consider this: If the Holy Spirit is praying through us with perfect prayer, wouldn't it seem reasonable to conclude that His prayers get results? You bet! What a Father! What a gift! Only He could have thought of it.

There are also the times when our faith falters and we feel far from God. The atmosphere is not right; the adversary is up to something, and we are floundering. I awoke in the night to this recently. I am so grateful I knew what to do. I went to one of my favorite verses in the little book of Jude where it says, "But you, beloved, building yourselves up on your most holy faith, praying in the Holy Spirit, keep yourselves in the love of God" (Jude 20, 21). So when I awoke and was troubled in the night, I prayed in my prayer language until the atmosphere changed, and I was strengthened.

Oh, it was so wonderful to cross that line from being weak to being built back up by the Holy Spirit! I prayed for a long time to reach that breakthrough—I am grateful I knew to pray until things changed. I knew not to quit until relief came by the Holy Spirit. Imagine all that was happening in the invisible realm when God Himself prayed for me, through me. Surely angels were involved. Did they "rough up" satan's minions, foiling their plans for me? Were satan's dark demons sent scrambling in disarray by mighty shining angels who were dispatched from the throne of God on my behalf? What I know for certain is that the spiritual climate changed, and I became strong again. I was built up in my faith and intensely aware of the love of God over me just as it says in Jude.

In addition to praying in tongues when we have a need, we can also use our prayer language when we praise God. Sometimes words aren't enough to praise Him sufficiently for His wonderful goodness. As we seek to lavish our love and praise on Him, we run out of words. It is so wonderful to pray and sing in a perfect language to Him, knowing we are giving glory to God beyond all that we are able to imagine or think. Now that is wonderful! Praising God perfectly—what a wonderful way to join our hearts and our voices with Heaven's celebration before the throne of God.

Prayer:

Wonderful Abba, Father, thank You for sending Your gift of the Holy Spirit. I need all the help I can get. I need empowering. I need to pray the perfect prayers You want to pray through me, and I need to be built up in my faith. Father, I need help keeping myself in the knowledge of your love instead of faltering in doubt. I open my heart to the Holy Spirit and say, "Come. Come to me as You came to the disciples on the Day of Pentecost."

MORE ABOUT THE WONDERFUL GIFT

"Peter said to them, 'Repent, and each of you be baptized in the name of Jesus Christ for the forgiveness of your sins; and you will receive the gift of the Holy Spirit. For the promise is for you and your children and for all who are far off, as many as the Lord our God will call to Himself'" (Acts 2:38-39).

"While Peter was still speaking these words, the Holy Spirit fell upon all those who were listening to the message. All the circumcised (Jewish)[63] believers who came with Peter were amazed, because the gift of the Holy Spirit had been poured out on the Gentiles also. For they were hearing them speaking with tongues and exalting God" (Acts 10:44-46).

The disciples were empowered on the Day of Pentecost, exactly as Jesus told them they would be. Peter was suddenly bold and fearless. Through the power of the Holy Spirit he got up and preached the gospel. As a result of his sermon, three thousand Jews received Jesus as Lord. Peter said to them,

---

[63] ( ) my note

"Repent, and each of you be baptized in the name of Jesus Christ for the forgiveness of your sins; and you will receive the gift of the Holy Spirit. For the promise is for you and your children and for all who are far off, as many as the Lord our God will call to Himself" (Acts 2:38, 39).

This was wonderful news. The gift of the Holy Spirit was part of the "package of salvation." It was promised to them, to their children and to the following generations as many as received Jesus. It was theirs to receive as soon as they repented and took Jesus as Lord.

Shortly thereafter, in Acts 10 and 11, we find the account of Peter going to Caesarea to Cornelius's house to preach the gospel. While Peter was still speaking to Cornelius and all who were gathered there, "The Holy Spirit fell upon all those who were listening to the message. All the circumcised believers who came with Peter were amazed, because the gift of the Holy Spirit had been poured out on the Gentiles also. They were hearing them speaking with tongues and exalting God" (Acts 10:44-46).

How did the Jews know the Spirit had been poured out on the Gentiles? Cornelius and his friends began speaking in a supernatural prayer language, the same way the Jews did on the Day of Pentecost.

This is wonderful news for the world. Salvation and the gift of the Holy Spirit with the evidence of praying in an unknown language is not only for the Jews who received Jesus, but for the Gentiles also. It was not only for the early church, but for all who believe on the Lord Jesus. It wasn't for a select few.

Our good Father made careful plans to ensure we would not be left like abandoned children when it was time for Jesus to return to Heaven. In reference to the Holy Spirit coming, Jesus said, "I will not leave you as orphans" (John 14:18). As a matter of fact, He said it was better for us for Him to go away: "But I tell you the truth, it is to your advantage that I go away;

for if I do not go away, the Helper will not come to you; but if I go, I will send Him to you" (John 16:7).

What a statement! It is better for us to have the Holy Spirit than for Jesus to physically walk the earth with us. Not one of us is to be left out. The promise of the Holy Spirit and the supernatural gift of His praying, through us and for us, with perfect praise and prayers is for all of us. What a way for God's children to bypass the corruption of the world and tap into the power of the supernatural kingdom of Heaven. What a way for us to become conduits of God's power as He continues to invade earth with the supernatural kingdom of God! What a crushing blow to the kingdom of darkness!

Nicky and I learned to use the power of praying in the Holy Spirit when we ministered in the Texas prisons. We were dealing with everything from satanists and mafia to murderers and rapists. Our work in such terrible darkness became powerful when we learned to pray for many hours in the Holy Spirit before we went to minister. Because of the Holy Spirit praying through us, we saw God demonstrate His power with signs, wonders, and miracles and many prisoners came to Christ.

When I received the gift of the Holy Spirit, I was reading a book written by a Jewish man who had become a Christian in the Jews for Jesus movement in the 1970s. In the last chapter he described how people had prayed for him to receive the Holy Spirit. I was a brand-new Christian, and in my mind I couldn't understand what on earth he was talking about. But in my heart I was desperate to have everything I could get from God. "I want this!" I cried out. A wonderful sensation came down on me as the Holy Spirit came upon me.

Later, some Christians explained to me about the gift of a prayer language. I learned I could speak in this heavenly language because I had prayed for the Holy Spirit to baptize me. They said to start praying, but not to use any English words. "Make sounds like a small child who is learning to talk." That seemed too simple. So feeling like a fool, but desperately hungry for more of God, I went home and prayed like a little child. I made little sounds. They came out each time as two syllables: ahh bahhh. Not feeling a thing, I gave up and decided to read my Bible. I randomly opened to a verse I had never seen before:

"For you did not receive the spirit of bondage again to fear, but you received the Spirit of adoption by whom we cry out, 'Abba, Father'" (Rom. 8:15). I was stunned. I had been saying "Abba". I had been saying "Daddy" in Aramaic!

Prayer:

Abba, Father, thank You that Your gift is for all of us. Thank You that You do not favor some of Your children over others. You are the perfect Father, and I adore You. The more I know You, the more I know there are not words to describe Your goodness and glory, except through the Holy Spirit. Help me appropriate all the power You intended for me when You sent the Holy Spirit. I give myself to You as an instrument of prayer in the name of Jesus.

CHAPTER 13

PRAYERS

PRAYERS EARLY IN THE MORNING

"O God, thou art my God; early will I seek thee: my soul thirsteth for thee, my flesh longeth for thee in a dry and thirsty land, where no water is. . . . My soul followeth hard after thee: thy right hand upholdeth me" (Psalm 63:1, 8, KJV).

"In the morning, O Lord, You will hear my voice; in the morning I will order my prayer to You and eagerly watch" (Psalm 5:3).

"With my soul have I desired thee in the night; yea, with my spirit within me will I seek thee early" (Isaiah 26:9, KJV).

Starting your day without praying early in the morning is like sending a horse through the starting gate of a race without warming him up first. He's not going to be in full stride. The whole day lies ahead of you; how you come out of the starting gate can determine how difficult or easy it will be to "run your race" for that day. Often the adversary is there when we awake. He offers us a barrage of trouble, trying to catch us off guard. He seeks to maneuver us out from under the protective wing of God first thing in the morning.

The Holy Spirit has not left us during the night, but He speaks in a still, small voice.[64] The adversary, on the other hand, shouts to us. We don't want to jump out of the "starting gate" of our day with him saddled on our back, yelling in our ear! We want to warm up with Jesus, first thing in the morning, before our race. In turn, we won't find ourselves running through "a dry and thirsty land" (Psalm 63:1).

For a good race, we must take time to listen to God and settle into His arms for the day. After Nicky left for Heaven I discovered this would take me hours instead of minutes, and it was worth the effort. I looked forward to hearing His instruction and being assured of His love. During that time the enemy was foiled as I cast off his worries and cares and put them in the hands of the Lord. In Psalm 63 David said, "Early will I seek thee. . . . My soul followeth hard after thee: thy right hand upholdeth me" (KJV). His language indicates real effort being applied, and his effort is rewarded. He breaks into praise, singing:

"Because thy lovingkindness is better than life, my lips shall praise thee. Thus will I bless thee while I live: I will lift up my hands in thy name. My soul shall be satisfied as with marrow and fatness; and my mouth shall praise thee with joyful lips" (Psalm 63:3-5, KJV). David had found the way to start the day.

---

[64] 1 Kings 19:12

Prayer:

O Father, I know I must seek You early. Help me. It is one thing to talk about pursuing You in the morning, but it is another thing to do it. So many things sound easy at first, and my flesh says, "I can do that." But then I run into my weaknesses that knock me flat. I have failed again and again. The only way I'm going to seek You early is with Your help and Your grace. I want to do it, Jesus, with all my heart. I want to turn to Your arms first thing every day as Your faithful one following hard after You. I ask for grace, my Lord. I ask for it now. Grace in the morning will greet me because You are faithful and living in me. Thank You, Jesus.

HEAVENLY PRAYERS IN THE NIGHT

"Who is this coming up from the wilderness leaning on her beloved?" (Song of Solomon 8:5a).

"But you, beloved, building yourselves up on your most holy faith, praying in the Holy Spirit, keep yourselves in the love of God, waiting anxiously for the mercy of our Lord Jesus Christ unto eternal life" (Jude 1:20-21).

"For a child will be born to us. . . and His name will be called. . .Prince of Peace" (Isaiah 9:6).

Going to bed at night can be the hardest part of being widowed. Even though I had prayed and come close to God before going to bed, I would often wake up in the middle of the night in great distress. This was not the time to shrink back and pull the covers over my head in retreat, because it would only get worse. It was time to lean on Jesus as in Song of Solomon 8:5, where it asks, "Who is this coming up from the wilderness leaning on her beloved?"

How do we lean on our beloved in the middle of the night? I start by saying the name of Jesus, calling on Him, and I start praying in my heavenly language. When the Holy Spirit is praying through me, the words of God are released into the darkness, and my faith is built up. For me, praying in the Holy Spirit is the fastest way to regain my footing. I mentioned this in chapter 12, but it bears repeating. I cannot imagine how I would have functioned without the gift of praying in tongues during some of my darkest hours after Nicky was gone.

Many times those darkest hours came in the middle of the night, testing everything within me. Jude 1:20 says that we are built up in our faith, we are kept in the love of God, and we are looking for His mercy as we pray in the Holy Spirit. Yes, mercy. God's compassion and relief are what I am looking for in the torment of an attack at night. While I pray in my prayer language, verses I have hidden in my heart are brought to mind by the Holy Spirit,[65] and my faith is built up. I am refreshed, being kept in the love of God. His love brings me up from the wilderness that was trying to engulf me. If the disturbance in the night is strong, I might have to stay awake for a while and read the Scriptures and worship until I find peace. Jesus is the Prince of Peace, and time with Him prevails over the darkness. An attack in the night is transformed into time spent with our Beloved instead. What a wonderful God we serve. Oh, how He loves us and welcomes us into His arms! His peace is wonderful.

Prayer:

O Jesus, how I want to be one who turns to Your embrace in the night hours. I want to cling to You and pursue the love and peace You offer me. Give me grace, Lord, never to allow separation even when caught off guard with interrupted sleep.

---

[65] See John 14:26.

Help me to flow freely in the release of the gift of my heavenly language. Father, I pray now for this gift You offer, designed to build me up and keep me in Your love. I want to be Your vessel releasing Holy Spirit prayer. I want to bring the voice of Heaven to earth even in the night watches.

WAKING TO A POUNDING STORM

"The floods have lifted up, O Lord, the floods have lifted up their voice, the floods lift up their pounding waves. More than the sounds of many waters, *than* the mighty breakers of the sea, the Lord on high is mighty" (Psalm 93:3, 4).

I woke up in a full panic in the middle of the night, paralyzing fear bearing down on me. My son was sick, and the doctors couldn't diagnose the problem. I had been praying for him and trusting God to take care of him, but now I was under a full demonic assault. Having lost my husband, the thought of losing my son came on me like a lion in the dark. My mind was racing with every frightening scenario of what might be wrong with him. I felt fear, thought fear and tasted fear, and my heart was racing. Unbelief raged at me, and angry accusations against God railed against my mind. "Lord, where are You?" I cried out. I was living Psalm 93:3: "The floods have lifted up, O Lord, the floods have lifted up their voice; the floods lift up their pounding waves."

It is one thing to preach, "Trust God," and it is another thing to do it when you are thrown into the middle of a surprise attack in the darkest hour of the night. I feebly tried to shake the panic by trying to praise, but the pressure mounted to a higher level as the accuser screamed, "You can't trust God. He's going to let the worst happen this time!"

I struggled to quote verses. "Jesus, You are my refuge and my fortress, my God in whom I trust."[66] The furious waves of fear and panic continued to buffet me until I arrived at the right place with the right cry to God. "Jesus, I can do nothing without You! It has to be You living in me to stand up against this! I can't praise, I can't pray, and I can't believe without You. Jesus, please live in me now!" The atmosphere shifted ever so slightly, and I was able to start praising and praying in the Spirit. I began quoting Scripture verses as the Lord brought them to my mind. I wrote down every concern and gave the list to God, casting my cares on Him.[67] Fear still crowded the room. But now, more than the mighty breakers of the sea that had crashed over me in the night, the presence and peace of the Lord began to flow into my darkness. Soon the siege was over. Yes, "the Lord on high is mighty!" He is mightier than any storm in the night.

Prayer:

Oh, Abba, Father, I surrender again to the absolute truth that apart from You I can do nothing. I must have Jesus living in me. Thank You that He does live in me and even helps me call for help. Oh, I worship You and thank You for Your faithfulness to be there always when I call. Thank You that You never leave me. You are my very present help in the time of trouble. I say yes to Psalm 93:4: "More than the sounds of many waters, than the mighty breakers of the sea, the Lord on high is mighty." Father, help me not lose sight of You, even in the worst storms. Help me not yield for a moment as the evil one tries to accuse You, to me. You are my Savior, the One who is mighty.

---

[66] See Ps. 91:2
[67] 1 Pet. 5:7

WHEN JESUS PRAYED ALONE ON THE MOUNTAIN

"But Jesus Himself would often slip away to the wilderness and pray" (Luke 5:16).

"It was at this time that He went off to the mountain to pray, and He spent the whole night in prayer to God" (Luke 6:12).

"And we know that God causes all things to work together for good to those who love God, to those who are called according to His purpose. For those whom He foreknew, He also predestined to become conformed to the image of His Son" (Romans 8:28, 29a).

I received three phone calls in one week from widows who were desperately lonely and struggling to make it through to some level of relief from their pain. Loneliness is painful. It can be excruciating. Their phone calls came while I was in the midst of my own struggle with my own isolation. There was some relief in getting a phone call from others in the same battle, but when you hang up the phone it is still there. As I lay on my bed praying for the two hours it took to pull out of my own nosedive, the sweet steady voice of the Holy Spirit came through. He said,

> "Margie, look at what is happening to you as you go through this."

So I reflected on my experience as a widow. Each stage I had been through had held levels of desperation that were inexpressible. So when the Lord said, "Look at what is happening to you," it took me aback at first, thinking He was pointing to something negative. But then I saw it.

When I got the phone calls from the widows I realized that I was sensitive to their cry. When I got off the phone I prayed for them with a depth of passion I did not possess for others before I was widowed. My intercession before the throne of grace was a desperation not for myself but for them—it was a loud cry for others to be bathed in grace—the grace and comfort that only He can give. Then my prayers expanded to a cry before God for all of suffering humanity. "O Father, how many are in despair tonight?" Then my prayer expanded even more to the ultimate cry, "Come, Lord Jesus, come. The Spirit and the bride say, 'Come, Lord Jesus, come.'" (see Rev. 22:17) I wasn't crying selfishly for Him to come just to relieve my own desperation, but I was praying with compassion for others. I was praying as Jesus prayed for the ultimate reconciliation of mankind to God.

Then it dawned on me. I had asked Jesus weeks ago, "What did You do when You stayed up all night praying? What was it like between You and the Father on the mountain?" He was answering my question. Through my suffering He was bringing me into that place He knew with the Father in intercession. I was being conformed to His image. Through my suffering the callousness of my own heart toward others was being scraped away. My deafness to the cries of others was being replaced with ears that hear and a heart that loves and is patient and inclined to listening to others in their need. This is how Jesus spent much of His time with the Father, as the Great High Priest interceding before the throne of God, pouring out the intercession of love and compassion for lost mankind. Then He went out in the power of God the next day delivering the love of the Father to the desperate and the lost.

Striking this cord of compassion in prayer is a very special place. It is a place in which our hearts are entwined with the heart of God and He is so pleased to find us there. While I am walking the path of the widow, I am finding that my prayers to be conformed to the image of Christ are being answered. I am going from glory to glory in the love of God.

Prayer:

Wonderful Father, open my eyes to the transformation I am going through. Help me see how You are at work in me. It is the truth that You cause all things to work together for good for those who love You. Help me see it and rejoice in You. Yes, help me see how You are changing me for Your glory.

CHAPTER 14

CONCLUSIONS

OH, BE QUIET!

I lay in bed with waves of dread rolling over me and buried my head in the pillow. Pushing dreadful thoughts away, I was in classic denial. Reality was too over-whelming to face.

I had already spent $9,000 making foundation repairs under the house. I had survived that disaster, and I found God very willing to get me through it. He had brought me all the help I needed.

After making it through the foundation repairs, I thought, "Surely there can't be any more catastrophes for me. I can sell this house and move into my new beginning." I had embraced the fact that my life as a widow was going to be a good and fruitful leg of my journey toward Heaven. Moving and starting over in life was the next step, but there I lay in bed, smothered by dread, hiding in denial.

Denial defies logic, and it is only a temporary door of escape. When I walked across the floor of my bedroom, I could feel the floor sinking and moving under my weight. I also saw it move, with cracks opening between the floor boards. These things would normally indicate there is a problem. But denial says, "No, this isn't happening."

I lay in bed, delaying getting up and putting my foot on the floor; denial was getting harder to hold on to. I had been on the phone with my son-in-law who had asked if I had seen the movie *The Money Pit*. It is a story about a young couple who watched the old house they were restoring collapse before their eyes. He was joking, trying to encourage me after my last home repair, thinking I was finished with my problems; at least *The Money Pit* was not my story. Little did he know my dreadful mornings.

Finally, I awoke one day and faced the fact that my house could not pass inspection, and I had to make repairs. Was it going to be thousands of dollars? I recalled the day I had crawled under the house and discovered the foundation had washed away. I remembered how I had cried bitter tears and failed to trust God. The Lord is so kind. His grace rolled over me, and He said,

> "This is your chance to trust Me and not be disappointed in yourself again. This is your chance to be pleasing to Me."

Well, I knew what pleased Him: Cast my care on Him, praise Him, rejoice and ask for His grace to do so. Trust Him to come through for me and lead me through the problem. Don't let go of hope or joy.

I bounded out of bed. "Jesus, give me grace!" I cried out. "I praise You, Father! I praise You, Father! I know You have the solution to this problem." My emotions were still raging, despite the fact that I was determined to trust God and watch Him work. I shouted, "Emotions, be quiet, and be quiet NOW! I am going to trust my Father as I go through this trial; pleasing Him is all I care about. My God is faithful to care for me, so BE QUIET!"

To my surprise, my emotions obeyed me! They stopped raging.

I had advanced instead of shrinking back, and I felt the Lord smiling over me. Nothing feels better.

Prayer:

Thank You, my Father. Pleasing You feels so good. I see it now, Lord. This is the road to total fearlessness. This is grace. You'll have me ready for whatever comes. I'll make it.

IT WAS WORTH IT

I was on the phone with a friend who had just been widowed. She was in turmoil. "Besides the terrible grief," she exclaimed, "with Al gone, I've developed an eating disorder, a sleeping disorder, an anxiety disorder, a mental disorder, an emotional disorder and a memory disorder!" In one statement she had put the entire "trauma syndrome" of her being widowed in a nutshell.

Nothing about her was functioning. She went on to say, "I miss my husband so much that I cry and cry. Being alone is terrible, and I'm afraid to be in this house by myself at night. The nighttime is the worst time of all. I can't sleep. I go to Walmart and shop all night to escape the torment of being in the house alone and grieving for Al. People say, "Get over it. You can't bring him back." They think I am crazy.

I was determined to be patient with her, and I assured her she wasn't losing her mind. As she continued on, I remembered the friend I had kept on the phone for hours in the middle of the night.

She went on to describe how she had fallen apart and cried uncontrollably in front of everyone at church. I was reminded of my own experience when I was at a dance class and they played a song that reminded me of my husband; I had to make a quick exit to avoid a meltdown in front of them. I had fled the room and sobbed into a corner in the hallway, trying to regain my composure.

I remembered all the people who meant well but said all the wrong things to me. There were those who thought it would help me to talk about my husband. They tried to guide me into conversations that I didn't want to have. My friend had the same experience, and we talked about extending grace to them and forgiving them.

I had been in a storm that didn't seem to have an end. Widows are surprised by how long it takes to become whole again. It is intimidating until you learn it is common for it to take years to heal. I found most people expected me to be recovered long before it was possible. This put pressure on me, so I was careful not to pressure my friend when she kept calling me late at night to "talk."

It was frightening to have been so dysfunctional. My hair was falling out, my weight was dropping, and I couldn't believe how gaunt and aged I looked in the mirror. I developed health problems and to my dismay, the siege advanced from weeks into months and then into years.

So I was glad to let my friend keep me up at night with her calls and to be there for her. She called about her neighbor stealing her husband's tools out of her shed and her not having the courage to confront him. I remembered the people who came on my land and stole things from my barn. Word was out that I was a widow.

My friend and I prayed together as she faced overwhelming problems. We watched while the Lord answered them, one by one, and she began to see that God was taking care of her. She had a flat tire on a back-country road, but some people came along and changed her tire for her, and then some friends invited her for Thanksgiving. Now it made sense why I had been through so much. It put me in a position to love my friend with a heart of understanding. I remembered the Lord's words to me:

> "How will you comfort My widows whose tears are hidden behind closed doors and never imagined by others, unless you experience it? Unless you travel in the hard places, how can you know, and how can you write and speak to those who are overwhelmed?"

I remembered how many times I lay on my bedroom floor, arms stretched out in surrender, my face toward Heaven, crying out, "Lord, please fix me." His Spirit would come, and I was blessed by His presence. But there were still missing parts. Finally, one day, as I stepped out of my closet, I was suddenly whole again. Amazing! I don't know how to describe it any better than to say I literally crossed over a line and knew I was no longer half a person. It was as though for three years God was gradually knitting me back together, and in that moment the final threads came together.

A friend told me she had the same experience four years after her husband died. I shared this experience with another friend, and she said, "Oh! Do you mean this feeling like half a person actually comes to an end?"

"Yes!"

As we walk with the Lord, He will restore us.

ABOUT THE AUTHOR

$\mathcal{M}$arjorie Osborne earned a BFA degree and Teacher's Certificate in Art when she graduated from Stephens College in 1971. Receiving Jesus Christ as her Savior shortly thereafter, she taught art in public school until she started her family. Applying her creative skills and her faith as a homemaker and mother of three, she eventually opened a home daycare for preschool children. For twenty years she loved being surrounded by toddlers, centering their creative activities on an awareness of Christ.

Her life took a turn in a new direction when she married her second husband, Nicky Osborne, in 1995. She became his ministry partner as he answered the call on his life to preach the gospel. Ministering in the Texas prisons and small churches, the Osbornes went anywhere God led them to share the good news of salvation through Jesus Christ. It was during those years that she developed her gift of writing by preparing materials and messages for the prisoners, as well as reports for those who interceded in prayer for the ministry. Soon she was writing devotionals as her love for God spilled out in written expression. Psalm 45:1 became a banner over her life: "My heart overflows with a good theme; I address my verses to the King; my tongue is the pen of a ready writer." After her beloved husband, Nicky, preceded her through the gates of Heaven, *The Widow's Might is Found at the Throne of Grace* became her first published work as a memorial to God's restoring power in the face of tragedy and loss.

CPSIA information can be obtained
at www.ICGtesting.com
Printed in the USA
FFOW01n1952010518
46423149-48266FF